THE ROASTING TIN
AROUND THE WORLD
GLOBAL ONE DISH DINNERS

FOR TEAM GLENGYLE: CHRISTINE, DANIELLE, EMMA AND LAURA.
AND, NOT LEAST, FOR ROSIE BRECKNER,
WITHOUT WHOM THIS BOOK WOULDN'T EXIST.

THE ROASTING TIN
AROUND THE WORLD

GLOBAL ONE DISH DINNERS

RUKMINI IYER

CONTENTS

USA
& THE CARIBBEAN

ATLANTIC
OCEAN

PACIFIC OCEAN

CENTRAL
& SOUTH AMERICA

ARCTIC OCEAN
EUROPE
& NORTH ASIA
ASIA
AFRICA
HE MIDDLE EAST
SOUTH EAST ASIA
& AUSTRALASIA
INDIAN OCEAN

INTRODUCTION

I was the kind of fifteen-year-old who took a few bites of a new dish on holiday and experienced the sort of heady rush that I'd later recognise in Remy from *Ratatouille*. Hollandaise sauce with salmon and asparagus in Mauritius – magical! A paella, cooked on an open flame at the table next to us in Granada, downing tiny cups of hot soup or interesting pastry confections pre-starter in Seville, taking pizza by the slice from an open window in Florence that was unlike any pizza I'd had before and realising in those moments that eating food abroad was the best thing. The only dish I remember returning was squid ink pasta in Rome – jet-black, complete with tentacles – ordered on the basis that sepia pasta, of which I'd never heard, sounded like a painting; what arrived didn't look like one. Visiting family in California, I could (and did) wander round supermarkets in a sort of ecstatic daze, admiring the perfect fresh produce just as much as the aisles of bright, unfamiliarly packaged biscuits, cereal and cake mix. Trips to India included my insistence on a return visit to a less than salubrious hotel in the South, on the basis that they had served the best doughnuts (cardamom scented; perfect) on a visit many years earlier. We arrived to find that they were no longer on the menu and this was met with howls. I was 23 years old. But I still think about those doughnuts.

Luckily for this book, my most dedicated attempts to Marie Kondo the house haven't shifted the drawerful of collected round-the-world recipes – some kitchen-smudged and handed over by harried but kind chefs, some beautifully typed up and presented in envelopes from hotels, and more recently scrawled down in my travel notebooks, as restaurants seem surprisingly unwilling to give out recipes to young women with an intent cheffy glint in their eye. So the Creole crab tarts on page 60 are the result of a trip to North Carolina, where I experimented as soon as we got home until I could recreate a tray of crab puffs from a favourite Cajun restaurant; the coconut rice and crispy chilli tofu (page 170) is inspired by a dish I had while travelling in Indonesia (OK, I'll admit it, it was a yoga retreat), and the shrimp and grits (page 56) are the result of trips to Tennessee and California, where it seems to be something of a hipster favourite. Perhaps the most delicious meatballs I've ever tasted were in a restaurant in St Petersburg, hence the Russian meatballs on page 200, and travelling through Beijing and Shanghai as a student was mind-expanding in learning about different types of Chinese cooking, some of which are included in the Asian chapter.

What I wanted to recreate in this *Roasting Tin* book was that feeling of amazement that I had in trying dishes from abroad for the first time, but presented in a way that was accessible for easy weeknight cooking. So this is a new collection of recipes that won't take any more effort than your average chop-and-chuck traybake, but will give you a whole new set of globally influenced flavours – some based on old favourites, like the steak and ale pie with mushrooms and rosemary on page 160, some rather more exotic, like the chermoula roasted tuna with raisins and peppers on page 134. As make-ahead cooking is as popular as ever, and as readers of the previous *Roasting Tin* books have noted how helpful it is to have recipes that you can pack for the working week, there are plenty in the following pages which are perfect to batch-cook for lunchboxes – the roasted broccoli with peas, butter beans and feta on page 210 and the pearl barley with rainbow vegetables and gremolata on page 140 are particular favourites. Similarly, most of my friends and many readers have fed back that they're always looking for new and interesting dishes to cook for their families and young children, so you'll find plenty of family-style traybakes and rice dishes – the mild Malaysian coconut roast chicken on page 158 and the lamb keema meatballs with lemon rice on page 108 are particularly child-friendly. And for those times when you're cooking for one, don't want leftovers and just want a gloriously crisp-topped tin to dive into for yourself, there's the salmon and broccoli pasta bake on page 72. As with my other books, almost all the ingredients are easily available at the supermarket, and in the case of the very small number of dishes that require specialist ingredients, the finished dish is so unusually good – like the pork pibil on page 26 and the Korean barbecued chicken on page 96 – that it's worth the minor inconvenience of buying from a specialist online retailer or even, dare I say it, Amazon.

Ovens are not the traditional cooking method of many of the food cultures in this book. As lots of readers will know, for Thai, Indian and other dishes, the spice-paste and onions are carefully fried in a pan until the oil separates before you're allowed to add any further ingredients. But I love the luxury of leaving food to cook itself without my attention, and didn't want to lose out on the incredible flavours that you get in recipes from these countries. It occurred to me that with dishes like the Thai beef panang with coconut and chilli on page 152 or the spiced paneer on page 98, you could coat the primary ingredient in a spice-paste, blast it in a hot oven to cook the spices, then quickly pour over any liquid ingredients for a final stint. But the citrus-spiked lamb, apricot and aubergine tagine on page 120 and the lime and coconut dal on page 100 are even easier, as the spices melt happily into the dishes without needing the two stages. While the authentic versions, which may require several pans and different steps, are unquestionably delicious, the idea behind converting these into one-tin dishes was as ever to make life easier on those days when you just don't have the time or inclination to stand in the kitchen stirring. When there are other things requiring attention – children, dogs, deadlines, friends arriving for dinner in twenty minutes – much as I love food and have a keen interest in traditional world cooking, if I can knock out a globally inspired dish that'll have family and friends amazed at the complexity of flavours, while I rather smugly know there's only one tin and a tableful of wineglasses to wash up after they've left, then I'll happily do that.

This book is a whistle-stop tour through dishes from around the world – I imagine it would be the size of *Encyclopaedia Britannica* were I able to convert every recipe into a tin format.

So I have limited myself to personal favourites, and those which work best in a roasting tin. Some dishes, like the Korean aubergines on page 106 and the jackfruit curry on page 88, are almost exactly how they'd taste traditionally, albeit made in the oven. Others are more loosely inspired – authentic Brazilian black beans are slow-cooked with garlic and onion until meltingly thick, then served with rice; in my version (page 30), the black beans, garlic and onion cook along with the rice in just 30 minutes, and I add a sharp lime, radish and avocado salsa to serve – perfect for a quick midweek meal or for lunchboxes. In case you find yourself eating one of the dishes and wanting to learn more about the food culture behind it, I've included a bibliography at the back for further reading which will point you in the direction of the authentic recipes from which I've drawn inspiration, along with cooking methods and fascinating stories from the countries covered in this book. I hope these recipes bring some of the excitement of travelling and trying new dishes into your kitchen, showing just what you can do with standard storecupboard ingredients, or, if you're feeling adventurous, one or two new ones. Raid the supermarket, dust off the spices from the back of the cupboard, and then, as ever, kick back and let the oven do the work.

A NOTE ON TINS

The key message is that you can use any kind. Pyrex lasagne dishes, ceramic dishes, the bottom half of a large Le Creuset, enamel tins, stainless steel tins, even the big tray that comes fitted in your oven as standard.

What you'll want to bear in mind is that you need to use a tin large enough for all your vegetables to fit in a single layer. If they pile up on top of each other, the ingredients underneath will steam, not roast, and may not cook in the time specified. Grains that go underneath the veg in stock aren't as fussy, and meat can sit on top of veg, if needed.

Most of the recipes in the book will suggest a size for the roasting tin in terms of fitting all the ingredients in one layer. I made pretty much everything except the cakes in my 30ish x 37cm roasting tins. If in doubt, go large.

A NOTE ON OVENS

Every oven is different. I was fascinated to learn that top oven manufacturers employ home economists to bake a tray of equally measured, standard British fairy cakes in their prototype ovens, to check for hot and cold spots depending on which cakes brown more, and then adjust the ovens accordingly to provide an even heat. (Sadly, I've never met one of these evenly browning ovens in real life, please advise if you have.) Cheffy types often use oven thermometers, which sit in your oven to tell you the exact temperature on the inside, which is almost always different from the temperature to which you turn the dial on the outside. (The oven in my mother's kitchen runs 10–20°C hotter than mine, so we often reduce either the temperature or the cooking time. The one at my sister's flat runs 10–20°C colder, so she usually adds 5–10 minutes to the cooking time.)

If you have an oven thermometer, by all means use it. But I don't think it's necessary to get too science-ey with roasting tin dinners. If you're already familiar with your oven, you may instinctively know to turn the dial up or down a bit more to allow for its foibles. If you're not a habitual oven user, it's easy enough to pick a simple recipe (cakes are good as it is very easy to objectively see how cooked they are within an allotted time), make a note of the results, then the next time adjust the temperature or cooking time up or down as needed.

All the recipes in my *Roasting Tin* books have been tested for oven timings in my oven at home, many in my mother's kitchen, a good proportion at friend's houses, an endearing number by the team at Penguin books and all of them in the oven where we shot the photographs you see in the book. If you find that the recipes consistently cook in more or less time in your oven, consider that it may be the oven and adjust the temperature or the timings as needed.

CENTRAL & SOUTH AMERICA

CENTRAL & SOUTH AMERICA

ROASTED SWEET POTATO WITH FETA,
SPRING ONIONS & PEANUTS (V)

SLOW-COOKED PORK PIBIL WITH PINK PICKLED ONIONS

CHIPOTLE ROASTED MUSHROOM & POTATO TACOS
(VEGAN)

ALL-IN-ONE BRAZILIAN BLACK BEANS
& RICE WITH AVOCADO & RADISH SALSA (VEGAN)

VENEZUELAN SLOW-COOKED BEEF
WITH RED PEPPERS & BAY

ROAST POTATOES, CHORIZO,
ONIONS & SOUR CREAM

ALL-IN-ONE BEEF CHILLI WITH CHOCOLATE

SMOKY CHIPOTLE CHICKEN
WITH BLACK BEANS, FETA & LIME

MEXICAN-STYLE ROAST PORK WITH ORANGE,
CUMIN & CINNAMON

SMOKY ROASTED SPROUTS & LEEKS
WITH FETA & THYME (V)

CUBAN-STYLE SWEET & SOUR SQUASH
WITH PEPPERS & BASIL (VEGAN)

PEACH & DULCE DE LECHE CAKE
WITH MERINGUES & CREAM (V)

ROASTED SWEET POTATO WITH FETA, SPRING ONIONS & PEANUTS

Roasted sweet potato is one of the easiest and nicest quick dinners I can think of, and this smoky version, jazzed up with sharp feta, spring onions and a good dose of crunch from the peanuts, is certainly among them. Add some freshly chopped red chilli if you like for extra heat.

Serves: 4
Prep: 10 minutes
Cook: 35–45 minutes

2 large sweet potatoes,
  cut into 2 1/2 cm wedges
  (you can peel them if you like
  – I leave the skin on)
1 red onion, quartered
2 tablespoons olive oil
2 teaspoons smoked paprika
1 teaspoon sea salt flakes
100g feta cheese, crumbled

DRESSING
2 tablespoons extra virgin olive oil
1 lime, zest and juice
1/2 teaspoon sea salt flakes,
  or to taste
3 spring onions, thinly sliced
A big handful of unsalted peanuts

TO SERVE
Sour cream or natural yogurt

Preheat the oven to 200°C fan/220°C/gas 7.

Tip the sweet potatoes, onion, oil, smoked paprika and sea salt into a roasting tin large enough to hold everything in one layer, then transfer to the oven and roast for 35–45 minutes (it's quicker if the potatoes are very fresh, and slower if they're a bit old).

Meanwhile, mix the extra virgin olive oil, lime zest and juice, sea salt if using, spring onions and peanuts together and set aside.

Once the sweet potatoes are cooked through, scatter over the spring onion dressing and the crumbled feta and serve hot, with sour cream or yogurt alongside.

SLOW-COOKED PORK PIBIL
WITH PINK PICKLED ONIONS

You may have had pork pibil at your favourite Mexican restaurant: it's a classic Yucatán dish of pork, slow-cooked in achiote, a paste made from annatto seeds, from which the dish gets its lovely colour. Achiote paste is easily available online, and once you have it, this dish will be a staple in your repertoire – it's so easy to put together.

Serves: 4
Prep: 10 minutes
Cook: 3 hours

1 onion, roughly chopped
6 cloves of garlic,
   roughly chopped
1 teaspoon ground cumin
1 tablespoon dried oregano
   (Mexican if you have it)
8 cloves
250ml orange juice
   (ideally freshly squeezed)
2 limes, juice only
50g achiote paste
2 teaspoons sea salt
800g free-range pork shoulder,
   diced

PICKLED ONIONS
½ red onion, very thinly sliced
1 lime, juice only

TO SERVE
Chopped fresh coriander
Tortillas and sour cream

Preheat the oven to 140°C fan/160°C/gas 2.

Tip the onion, garlic, cumin, oregano, cloves, citrus juice, achiote paste and salt into a blender or food processor and blitz until smooth.

In a small deep roasting tin or lidded casserole dish, mix the pork shoulder with the spice paste. Cover tightly with foil or the lid, then transfer to the oven and cook for 3 hours.

Meanwhile, mix the very thinly sliced red onion with the lime juice and set aside for 3 hours, stirring occasionally. (The acid in the lime juice will turn the onions a beautiful bright pink by the time the pork is ready.)

Once cooked, remove the foil or lid and shred the pork while hot. Serve with the pink pickled onions, chopped coriander, warm tortillas and sour cream.

Note: This dish isn't at all spicy, so it's a good one for kids, and can be easily made ahead, frozen and defrosted in portions.

CHIPOTLE ROASTED MUSHROOM & POTATO TACOS

I fully approve of carb on carbs for dinner, and these smoky spiced potatoes, mushrooms and tomatoes work beautifully with tacos against the sour cream, lime and tortillas. Serve as part of a sharing feast on taco night or with warm tortillas for an easy midweek dinner.

Serves: 2–3
Prep: 10 minutes
Cook: 45 minutes

450g large chestnut mushrooms, whole, a few halved
650g Charlotte potatoes, quartered
250g cherry tomatoes
3 tablespoons olive oil
2 teaspoons ground cumin
1 tablespoon coriander seeds, lightly crushed
1 teaspoon chipotle chilli flakes
2 teaspoons sea salt flakes
A big handful of fresh thyme
1 lime, juice only

TO SERVE
150g vegan yogurt or sour cream
Warm tortillas

Preheat the oven to 200°C fan/220°C/gas 7.

Tip the mushrooms, potatoes, tomatoes, oil, spices, salt and thyme into a roasting tin large enough to hold everything in one layer, then transfer to the oven and roast for 45 minutes.

Squeeze over the lime juice, adjust the salt to taste and serve piled into tortillas with the vegan sour cream or yogurt.

ALL-IN-ONE BRAZILIAN BLACK BEANS & RICE WITH AVOCADO & RADISH SALSA

Traditionally, Brazilian black beans are slow-cooked with garlic, onions and sometimes a little bacon, then served on top of fluffy white rice for a comforting, filling dinner. In this vegan version, I cook the beans, garlic and rice together to save on cooking pots, and a quick, fresh avocado, coriander and radish salsa finishes the dish off along with a handful of crunchy salted peanuts.

Serves: 4
Prep: 10 minutes
Cook: 30 minutes

200g basmati rice
500ml vegetable stock
200g spring greens, thinly sliced
2 cloves of garlic, grated
2 x 400g tins of black beans,
   drained and rinsed
2 shallots, thinly sliced

SALSA
100g fresh coriander,
   roughly chopped
200g radishes, quartered
100ml olive oil
2 limes, juice and zest
1 teaspoon sea salt flakes
2 firm avocados,
   cut into 2cm pieces

TO SERVE
2 handfuls of salted peanuts

Preheat the oven to 210°C fan/230°C/gas 8.

Tip the rice, stock, spring greens, garlic and black beans into a medium lidded casserole dish or roasting tin, then scatter over the sliced shallots. Cover with the lid or very tightly with foil (this is important so the rice cooks through), then transfer to the oven and cook for 30 minutes.

Meanwhile, mix the coriander, radishes, olive oil, lime juice, zest and sea salt together, then gently stir through the avocado pieces. Adjust the salt to taste.

Once the rice is cooked, fluff it through with a fork, then stir through half of the avocado salsa. Taste, adjust the salt as needed, then scatter over the remaining salsa and the peanuts and serve hot.

VENEZUELAN SLOW-COOKED BEEF
WITH RED PEPPERS & BAY

This dish of slow-cooked beef is known as *ropa vieja* in Cuba –
rather unromantically translating as 'old rope', on account of how
the beef looks when shredded into long strands. The Venezuelan
version below includes red peppers and tomatoes: they're usually
fried and added at the end, but I love the flavour you get from
cooking them alongside the beef. Bavette or skirt steak is a must
here – it becomes meltingly tender after a long, slow cook, and
for so few ingredients, this is really something special.

Serves: 4
Prep: 15 minutes
Cook: 2 hours 20 minutes

4 beef bavette or skirt steaks
    (approx. 180g each)
3 red peppers, thickly sliced
2 white onions, thickly sliced
2 tablespoons olive oil
1 teaspoon sea salt flakes
500ml boiling beef stock
3 large tomatoes, diced
1 tablespoon
    Worcestershire sauce
1 teaspoon ground cumin
2 bay leaves

TO SERVE
Fresh flat-leaf parsley, chopped
Rice and black beans

Preheat the oven to 200°C fan/220°C/gas 7.

Tip the steaks, peppers and onions into
a medium sized roasting tin or a large flat
lidded casserole dish with the oil and salt –
it's OK if the steak sits on top of the peppers.
Mix well, then transfer to the oven for
20 minutes.

Once the steak has had 20 minutes and the
peppers are just beginning to soften, take
the dish out of the oven and add the stock,
tomatoes, Worcestershire sauce, cumin and
bay leaves. Cover tightly with foil or a lid and
transfer to the oven for 2 hours, reducing the
temperature to 160°C fan/180°C/gas 4.

After 1 hour and 15 minutes, remove the foil or
lid and let the dish bubble down uncovered for
the final 45 minutes.

Let it sit for 10 minutes, then shred the beef
with two forks while still warm. Scatter with
parsley and serve alongside rice and beans.

ROAST POTATOES, CHORIZO, ONIONS & SOUR CREAM

This is a lovely dish to pile into warm tortillas, or just to have by itself for a warming weeknight dinner. The chorizo crisps up on the top, while giving flavour and body to the lightly golden potatoes – not bad for a dish you can make with a few storecupboard ingredients.

Serves: 4
Prep: 10 minutes
Cook: 40–45 minutes

600g potatoes
   (e.g. Maris Piper, Desiree),
   peeled and cut into 2cm cubes
260g chorizo, thickly sliced
   into 2cm pieces
2 white onions, thickly sliced
1 tablespoon olive oil
A handful of fresh thyme
2 bay leaves
250ml chicken stock

TO SERVE
A handful of fresh coriander,
   roughly chopped
150ml sour cream
   or natural yogurt

Preheat the oven to 200°C fan/220°C/gas 7.

Tip the potatoes, chorizo, onions, oil, thyme and bay leaves into a roasting tin large enough to hold everything in one layer, and mix well.

Pour in the chicken stock, then transfer to the oven and roast for 45–50 minutes, until the potatoes are golden brown and cooked through and the stock is absorbed.

Taste the potatoes and adjust the salt as needed (they should be fine, on account of the chorizo and stock), then scatter over the coriander and serve with the sour cream or yogurt.

ALL-IN-ONE BEEF CHILLI WITH CHOCOLATE

I could live off this Mexican inspired chilli – and have been known to, given that it makes enough to feed a crowd with more to spare. This chilli uses brisket, along with a little diced pork shoulder for richness. If you are a spice aficionado, by all means add a couple of guajillo chillies and a mulato chilli if you have them, but this is just as lovely with the more readily available chipotle and ancho chillies.

Serves: 6
Prep: 15 minutes
Cook: 3 hours

1 teaspoon ground cumin
1 onion, roughly chopped
2 cloves of garlic, thinly sliced
800g beef brisket,
   cut into 2½ cm chunks
350g pork shoulder,
   cut into 2½ cm chunks
1 ancho chilli
2 teaspoons chipotle chilli flakes
2 teaspoons ground coriander
2 teaspoons ground cumin
2 teaspoons smoked paprika
1 x 400g tin of tomatoes
600ml beef stock
A large pinch of sea salt
10g dark chocolate
   (minimum 70% cocoa solids)

TO SERVE
Sour cream, fresh coriander
   and tortilla chips

Preheat the oven to 150°C fan/170°C/gas 3.

Tip all the ingredients apart from the salt and chocolate into a deep roasting tin or lidded casserole dish and stir. Cover tightly with foil or a lid, then transfer to the oven and cook for 3 hours.

Once cooked, shred the meat with two forks, then stir in the chocolate and season with sea salt. Stir in a spoonful of sour cream, scatter over the coriander and serve with tortilla chips and the rest of the sour cream.

Notes: Like most stews, this will taste even better after a night in the fridge. For make-ahead meals or batch-cooking, this is very easy to freeze and defrost in portions as needed.

SMOKY CHIPOTLE CHICKEN
WITH BLACK BEANS, FETA & LIME

I love the combination of flavours and textures in this dish: the sharp, lime-spiked black beans and feta against the spiced chicken, with hits of salt from the chorizo and texture from the sweetcorn. My favourite sort of dish – simple enough to have on a weeknight, smart enough to make for friends.

Serves: 4
Prep: 15 minutes
Cook: 1 hour

1 red onion, quartered
3 cloves of garlic, unpeeled
4 corn on the cob
8 free-range chicken thighs
150g chorizo, roughly chopped
3 teaspoons chipotle chilli flakes
1 teaspoon sea salt
2 teaspoons ground coriander
2 tablespoons olive oil
A handful of fresh coriander,
  chopped

SALSA
1 x 400g tin of black beans,
  drained and rinsed
2 tablespoons extra virgin olive oil
100g feta cheese, crumbled
2 limes, juice and zest

Preheat the oven to 180°C fan/200°C/gas 6.

Tip the onion, garlic, corn, chicken and chorizo into a roasting tin large enough to hold everything in one layer (you may need to use two medium tins), then add the chilli flakes, sea salt, ground coriander and olive oil and work them into the chicken and sweetcorn.

Transfer the tin(s) to the oven and roast for 1 hour, until the chicken is golden brown and cooked through.

Meanwhile, mix the black beans, extra virgin olive oil, feta, lime juice and zest in a bowl and set aside. Once the chicken has come out of the oven, scatter over the black bean salsa and coriander, and serve hot.

MEXICAN-STYLE ROAST PORK
WITH ORANGE, CUMIN & CINNAMON

This is one of the nicest dishes of pulled pork I've ever made, and the recipe was inspired by watching Mexican chef Cristina Martinez on *Chef's Table*. While a home cook with an ordinary oven can't hope to create anything like the slow-cooked miracle that is her barbacoa, this version is unlikely to disappoint your guests.

Serves: 6–8
Prep: 10 minutes
Cook: 4 hours 30 minutes

2 white onions, thickly sliced
1/2 bulb garlic, cloves
   crushed but unpeeled
2 oranges, thickly sliced
2 bay leaves
2 teaspoons fresh
   or dried oregano
1 large cinnamon stick
2kg boned pork shoulder
2 teaspoons sea salt
3 teaspoons ground cumin
1 tablespoon freshly ground
   black pepper

TO SERVE
Tortillas and sour cream
Chilli sauce (optional)

Preheat the oven to 140°C fan/160°C/gas 2.

Tip the onions, garlic, oranges, bay leaves, oregano and cinnamon stick into a large lidded casserole dish or a roasting tin. Rub the pork shoulder all over with the sea salt, ground cumin and pepper, then sit the pork on top of the vegetables (you may need to move the vegetables and orange slices around so some sit around the pork joint in order to fit it into your casserole dish).

Cover tightly with foil or the lid, then transfer to the oven and roast for 4 hours 30 minutes. Remove the lid or foil for the final 45 minutes and increase the oven temperature to 200°C fan/220°C/gas 7, to allow the skin to crisp up.

Remove the crackling and cut it into pieces. Shred the cooked pork with two forks, and serve the pork and crackling with tortillas, sour cream and your favourite chilli sauce, if you wish.

SMOKY ROASTED SPROUTS & LEEKS WITH FETA & THYME

This is such a quick and easy filling for tortillas – the leeks go all melty, the sprouts crisp up, and the flavour of baked feta and thyme against both makes this a moreish regular at my dinner table. I'd suggest this along with the chipotle mushrooms and potatoes on page 28 if you're doing a vegetarian taco night.

Serves: 4
Prep: 10 minutes
Cook: 35–40 minutes

2 large leeks, cut diagonally
  into 2cm slices
350g Brussels sprouts, halved
1 red onion, cut into eighths
2 tablespoons olive oil
2 teaspoons smoked paprika
100g feta, crumbled
A large handful of fresh
  lemon thyme

DRESSING
1 tablespoon extra virgin olive oil
1 tablespoon lemon juice
A pinch of sea salt flakes

TO SERVE
A handful of fresh coriander
  leaves
Warm tortillas
Sour cream or natural yogurt

Preheat the oven to 180°C fan/200°C/gas 6.

Tip the leeks, sprouts and red onion into a roasting tin large enough to hold them all in one layer, then stir through the olive oil and smoked paprika. Scatter over the feta and thyme, then transfer to the oven and roast for 35–40 minutes, until the sprouts and leeks are cooked through and are just turning golden brown.

Mix together the extra virgin olive oil, lemon juice and salt, and pour all over the vegetables. Taste and adjust the lemon juice and salt as needed, then scatter over the coriander. Serve with warm tortillas and sour cream or yogurt.

CUBAN-STYLE SWEET & SOUR SQUASH WITH PEPPERS & BASIL

In this Cuban dish, a simple mix of vinegar, sugar, garlic and ginger really brings out the flavour of the squash. If you can find cubanelle rather than ordinary pointed peppers (they're a bit like the long pale green peppers that you can get in Asian grocery stores), then by all means use those instead. I like this as part of a spread of vegetable dishes.

Serves: 4–6
Prep: 15 minutes
Cook: 1 hour 10 minutes

1 butternut squash,
  cut into eighths
4 pointy peppers, mixed colours
2 red onions, halved
4 cloves of garlic, grated
8cm ginger, grated
1 teaspoon chilli flakes
2 teaspoons caster sugar
60ml white vinegar
60ml water
2 tablespoons olive oil
Sea salt flakes
Extra virgin olive oil
A handful of pumpkin seeds
A large bunch of fresh basil

TO SERVE
Rice and (vegan) sour cream

Preheat the oven to 180°C fan/200°C/gas 6.

Tip the squash, peppers and onions into a roasting tin large enough to hold everything in one layer (it's OK if the onions sit on top). Mix the garlic, ginger, chilli flakes, caster sugar, vinegar, water and oil in a small bowl, then pour this over the vegetables and mix well.

Cover the roasting tin tightly with foil, then transfer to the oven and cook for 45 minutes. After that, remove the foil, turn the temperature up to 200°C fan/220°C /gas 7, and roast for a further 15–20 minutes, until the peppers get a good colour on them (the undersides of the squash will caramelise, but the top will not).

Remove the dish from the oven, taste the squash and peppers and adjust the salt as needed. Drizzle with a little good extra virgin olive oil, then scatter over the pumpkin seeds and basil and serve with rice and (vegan) sour cream.

PEACH & DULCE DE LECHE CAKE
WITH MERINGUES & CREAM

In Uruguay, the original version of this cake is known as *chajá* – layers of light, fluffy sponge soaked in peach syrup, whipped cream, dulce de leche, peach slices and crumbled meringue. My version incorporates the dulce de leche and fresh peaches into an olive oil cake – serve it warm out of the oven, with crème fraîche or lightly whipped cream alongside.

Serves: 8
Prep: 15 minutes
Cook: 25 minutes

225g olive oil
225g dulce de leche
   (you can use tinned Nestlé
   caramel, sold next to the
   condensed milk)
50g caster sugar
4 free-range eggs
225g self-raising flour
1 teaspoon baking powder
3 under- to just-ripe peaches,
   thinly sliced

TO SERVE
175g dulce de leche
   (this is the remaining
   caramel in the tin)
A handful of crushed
   shop-bought meringues
Crème fraîche or lightly
   whipped cream

Preheat the oven to 160°C fan/180°C/gas 4.

In a food processor or by hand, mix the olive oil and dulce de leche together with the sugar until well combined, then beat in the eggs, one at a time. Fold in the flour and baking powder, then pour into a 26cm by 20cm roasting tin or cake dish.

Arrange the sliced peaches over the batter, then transfer to the oven and bake for 25 minutes, until golden brown and a skewer inserted into the middle comes out clean.

Let the cake cool in the tin for 10 minutes. Melt the remaining dulce de leche in a pan until smooth and pourable, then drizzle this over the warm cake. Scatter with a handful of crushed meringues, then serve with crème fraîche or lightly whipped cream alongside.

Notes: As this cake contains fresh fruit, if you are not eating it on the day you make it, store it in the fridge. I like to warm it up slice by slice in the microwave – 30 seconds on high.

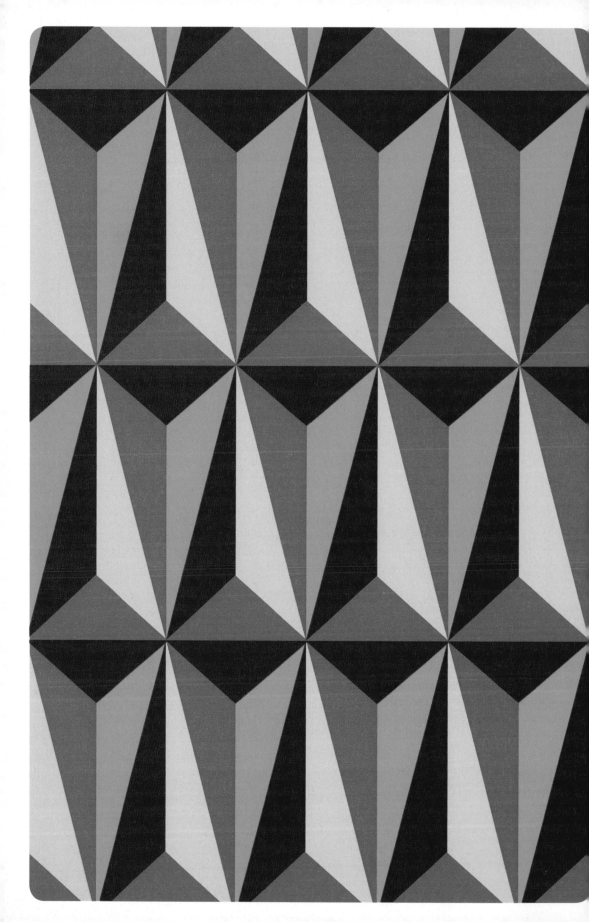

USA
& THE CARIBBEAN

USA & THE CARIBBEAN

BAKED POLENTA WITH PRAWNS
(SHRIMP & GRITS)

BUFFALO CAULIFLOWER 'WINGS'
WITH BLUE CHEESE & CELERY (V)

CREOLE SPICED CRAB TARTS
WITH LEMON & CHILLI

BAKED AVOCADO WITH WALNUTS, BLUE CHEESE
& HONEY (V)

SMOKY SAUSAGE CASSEROLE
WITH CHORIZO, PEPPERS & BEANS

JERK CHICKEN WITH SWEET POTATO, PINEAPPLE & LIME

CRISPY KALE & BACON MAC & CHEESE

CRISPY BAKED SQUASH GRATIN WITH PARMESAN & LEEKS (V)

SALMON, BROCCOLI & SPINACH PASTA BAKE

BARBECUE STYLE RIBS
WITH NEW POTATOES, SOUR CREAM & CHIVES

S'MORES ROCKY ROAD WITH PEANUTS,
MARSHMALLOWS & CHOCOLATE (V)

BAKED POLENTA WITH PRAWNS (SHRIMP & GRITS)

I could not stop ordering shrimp and grits on my last visit to the USA – it's the most wonderful savoury polenta-like dish, packed with cheese, and topped with spicy, garlicky prawns. Polenta is easier to buy than the slightly coarser cornmeal used for grits, so I have substituted it here for ease.

Serves: 2
Prep: 10 minutes
Cook: 30 minutes

150g quick-cook polenta
75g mature Cheddar
400ml chicken stock
1 small leek, thinly sliced
20g fresh flat-leaf parsley,
   finely chopped
150g raw king prawns
1/2 teaspoon chipotle chilli flakes
1 tablespoon olive oil
1/2 teaspoon sea salt flakes
200g vine cherry tomatoes,
   halved
1/2 lemon, juice only

Preheat the oven to 200°C fan/220°C/gas 7.

Tip the polenta, Cheddar, chicken stock, leek and half the parsley into a small roasting tin and stir. Transfer to the oven and cook for 20 minutes.

Meanwhile, mix together the prawns, chilli flakes, olive oil, sea salt and halved cherry tomatoes and set aside.

Take the polenta out of the oven after 20 minutes and top with the prawns and tomatoes in an even layer. Return the tin to the oven for 10 minutes, until the prawns are pink and cooked through. Squeeze over the lemon juice, adjust the salt to taste, scatter over the remaining parsley and serve hot.

BUFFALO CAULIFLOWER 'WINGS' WITH BLUE CHEESE & CELERY

This dish is inspired by Niki Segnit's recipe for buffalo chicken wings in *The Flavour Thesaurus* – and I'm not ashamed to say that I ate the entire contents of this vegetarian version when it came out of the oven. The Stilton and yogurt dip is just addictive with the crisp spice-butter roasted cauliflower – perfect to serve to friends with drinks for a casual get-together.

Serves: 2–3 as a snack
Prep: 10 minutes
Cook: 25 minutes

30g salted butter
2 cloves of garlic, grated
1 teaspoon cayenne pepper
1 teaspoon smoked paprika
1 teaspoon sea salt flakes
1 cauliflower, cut into
   medium florets
Cauliflower greens,
   cut down to bite-size pieces

DIP
60g natural yogurt
30g Stilton, crumbled
   (I like Long Clawston)

TO SERVE
Celery sticks, thinly sliced

Preheat the oven to 180°C fan/200°C/gas 6.

You'll need a roasting tin big enough for all the cauliflower florets to sit in, but before you stick them in the tin, put the butter and garlic into the tin and pop it into the oven for 2–3 minutes, until the butter has just melted.

Tip the cayenne pepper, smoked paprika and sea salt into the melted butter, give it a stir, then add the cauliflower florets and greens. Work the spiced butter really well into the cauliflower, then transfer to the oven and roast for 25 minutes, until the cauliflower is crisp and just cooked through.

Meanwhile, mix together the yogurt and Stilton and set aside. Serve the wings hot, with the blue cheese dip and celery sticks alongside.

CREOLE SPICED CRAB TARTS
WITH LEMON & CHILLI

I first had these crab tarts in a restaurant on a US road trip, and found them so addictive that I wrote down everything I could remember about them as soon as I got back to the hotel. Several re-creations later and I was happy with this version – they're perfect as a dinner party starter, for a light lunch or supper with a salad, or even for lunchboxes. The secret ingredient? Tinned crab – by all means use fresh if you prefer, but tinned makes no discernible difference under all the hot sauce and garlic.

Serves: 4
Prep: 15 minutes
Cook: 25–30 minutes

180g Philadelphia
½ teaspoon paprika
2–4 tablespoons of your
   favourite hot sauce
   (I like to non-canonically use
   sriracha, but D. L. Jardine's
   Texas Champagne is lovely)
1 large clove of garlic, grated
½ red onion, finely chopped
½ lemon, juice only
2 x 145g tins of jumbo crabmeat,
   drained
1 x 420g sheet of puff pastry
   (all-butter if you can find it)
A handful of finely grated
   Parmesan
A handful of white breadcrumbs

TO SERVE
A little finely chopped fresh
   flat-leaf parsley

Preheat the oven to 180°C fan/200°C/gas 6.

In a large bowl, mix the Philadelphia, paprika, hot sauce, garlic, onion and lemon juice, then gently stir through the crabmeat. Taste, and adjust the hot sauce as you wish. (The lid accidentally fell off my bottle of sriracha once and it didn't do any harm, so be generous.)

Lay your puff pastry out on a baking sheet or in a shallow roasting tin, and cut it into 8 squares. Divide the crab mix equally between the pieces of pastry and spread it out, leaving a 1cm border at the edges. Scatter each tart with a little Parmesan and breadcrumbs, then transfer to the oven to cook for 25–30 minutes, until the pastry is golden brown and crisp.

Scatter with flat-leaf parsley, and serve hot.

Note: These keep well in the fridge to serve the following day, and if you're dying of hunger, 40 seconds in the microwave will do rather than waiting for the oven to reheat.

BAKED AVOCADO WITH WALNUTS, BLUE CHEESE & HONEY

This is my nod to the classic eighties dish of stuffed avocado, which I always think of as very American after reading *The Bell Jar* as a teenager. Helpfully, this version has no crabmeat – it's a combination of the baked avocado stuffed with blue cheese and bacon which I had in Tennessee, and the (unbaked) version my mother used to make when I was younger with raisins, walnuts and Philadelphia.

Serves: 4
Prep: 10 minutes
Cook: 10–15 minutes

100g walnuts
100g Roquefort
   or vegetarian blue cheese
125g yogurt
75g raisins
4 avocados, halved and stoned
A pinch of smoked paprika
   or cayenne
Chopped flat-leaf parsley
100g baby leaf spinach

DRESSING
1 tablespoon olive oil
1/2 lemon, juice only
1 tablespoon honey
A pinch of sea salt flakes,
   to taste

Preheat the oven to 180°C fan/200°C/gas 6.

Mix together the walnuts, cheese, yogurt and raisins and stuff the mixture into the halved avocados. Pop them into a roasting tin large enough to hold them all neatly and bake for 10–15 minutes, until the topping is just golden brown.

Meanwhile, whisk the olive oil, lemon juice and honey together with a little pinch of sea salt flakes. Just before serving, scatter the smoked paprika or cayenne and parsley over the avocados, toss the dressing through the spinach, and serve alongside.

Note: If you aren't a fan of blue cheese, you can substitute feta, or indeed Philadelphia.

SMOKY SAUSAGE CASSEROLE
WITH CHORIZO, PEPPERS & BEANS

If you remember having tinned spaghetti hoops with sausages when you were a child and haven't had them since, you are in for a treat. This recipe for homemade baked beans with sausages – packed with herbs, peppers and chorizo – can disguise itself under the name of a smoky sausage casserole, but it's still unmistakably nostalgic children's food, and all the better for it.

Serves: 4
Prep: 15 minutes
Cook: 50 minutes

1 red pepper, thinly sliced
1 yellow pepper, thinly sliced
1 orange pepper, thinly sliced
1 red onion, roughly sliced
12 free-range pork chipolatas
100g chorizo from a ring,
    cut into 1 1/2 cm slices
3 sprigs of fresh rosemary
3 bay leaves
1 tablespoon olive oil
1 teaspoon sea salt
Freshly ground black pepper
1 x 400g tin of haricot beans,
    drained
2 x 400g tins of chopped
    tomatoes
400ml boiling water

Preheat the oven to 200°C fan/220°C/gas 7.

Tip the peppers, onion, sausages, chorizo, rosemary, bay leaves, olive oil, sea salt and a good grind of pepper into a roasting tin large enough to hold everything in one layer – use the biggest tin you have.

Mix well, then transfer to the oven and roast for 25 minutes, until the sausages are just starting to brown.

Stir in the haricot beans, chopped tomatoes and boiling water, then return to the oven for a further 20–25 minutes. If you've used a nice big roasting tin, the sauce will have reduced and the sausages will have browned off nicely – you may need to cook it for a further 10 minutes in a smaller roasting tin to reduce the tomato sauce.

Serve with good crusty bread. This tastes even better the next day, and freezes very well.

JERK CHICKEN WITH SWEET POTATO, PINEAPPLE & LIME

This is my version of jerk chicken, and I would happily eat it every week at home when nipping down to Brixton isn't on the cards. The roasted pineapple provides sweetness against the sharpness of the lime, with spiced sweet potato as the carb. Easy enough to make on a weeknight, nice enough to make for friends at the weekend.

Serves: 4
Prep: 5 minutes
Cook: 1 hour

2 sweet potatoes,
  cut into quarters
1 red onion, cut into quarters
1kg free-range chicken thighs
  and drumsticks (2 per person)
8 slices of fresh pineapple
  (ready-prepared if you wish)
2 limes, halved
3 teaspoons jerk seasoning
3 teaspoons demerara sugar
3 cloves of garlic, grated
3 tablespoons olive oil
1 teaspoon sea salt flakes

TO SERVE
Finely chopped coriander
Sour cream or natural yogurt

Preheat the oven to 170°C fan/190°C/gas 5.

Tip the sweet potatoes, onion, chicken, pineapple and limes into a roasting tin big enough to hold them in one layer, then mix everything well with the jerk seasoning, demerara sugar, grated garlic and olive oil. Scatter everything evenly with the sea salt flakes, making sure to get plenty on the chicken skin, then transfer to the oven and roast for 1 hour.

After 1 hour, remove the tin from the oven and let the chicken rest for 5–10 minutes. Squeeze the juice from the roasted limes over everything, taste and adjust the salt as needed, scatter with a little fresh coriander and serve hot. It's non-canonical, but I like this with sour cream or yogurt alongside.

CRISPY KALE & BACON MAC & CHEESE

The dish opposite didn't last very long after we took the photograph, mostly because I was stealing hot pieces of crisp bacon from the top. It's a quick weeknight win, and popular with children – crème fraîche makes for an easy béchamel sauce sauce substitute.

Serves: 4
Prep: 15 minutes
Cook: 25 minutes

300g macaroni
200g kale/Swiss chard, thinly sliced
150g mature Cheddar, grated
500g crème fraîche
A pinch of sea salt flakes
2 teaspoons smooth Dijon mustard
90g bacon or pancetta lardons
60g white or panko breadcrumbs

Preheat the oven to 180°C fan/200°C/gas 6.

Tip the macaroni into a pan of boiling, salted water and cook for 10 minutes, or until just al dente. Tip in the kale or Swiss chard for the last minute, then drain well.

Stir three-quarters of the Cheddar, the crème fraîche, sea salt and mustard through the hot pasta and kale, then transfer to a roasting tin. Scatter over the remaining cheese, bacon lardons and panko breadcrumbs, then transfer to the oven and bake for 20 minutes, until the topping is golden brown and crisp. Serve hot.

CRISPY BAKED SQUASH GRATIN WITH PARMESAN & LEEKS

This is perfect for an autumnal dinner with some good bread alongside – the almond and Parmesan crust works beautifully against the sage-infused cream, leeks and squash. It's quite rich, so I like to serve it with a simply dressed lemon and spinach salad.

Serves: 4
Prep: 15 minutes
Cook: 1 hour

500g butternut squash,
   peeled and very thinly sliced
1 leek, thinly sliced
8 fresh sage leaves
1 teaspoon sea salt flakes
Freshly ground black pepper
350g crème fraîche
150ml vegetable stock
30g vegetarian Parmesan, grated
15g fresh flat-leaf parsley,
   finely chopped
30g flaked almonds,
   roughly chopped

Preheat the oven to 180°C fan/200°C/gas 6.

Mix the squash, leek, sage, sea salt and pepper in a medium roasting tin, then spread the crème fraîche over the top. Pour over the vegetable stock, smooth everything down with a spoon, then transfer to the oven and bake for 1 hour.

Mix together the Parmesan, parsley and almonds. After 45 minutes, remove the roasting tin from the oven, scatter the Parmesan mixture all over the squash, then return to the oven for a further 15 minutes, until the squash is cooked through, and the topping is crisp. Serve hot.

Note: You will need to cut the squash very thinly to cook through in 1 hour – if you have sliced it more thickly, it will take longer if the oven.

SALMON, BROCCOLI & SPINACH PASTA BAKE

I couldn't write a book without another salmon and broccoli recipe, and this version, inspired by the Italian-American classic 'baked ziti' is one of the nicest. I particularly like that this recipe serves one. It is best eaten greedily and immediately, and there's something rather nice about having a tin to oneself. But do scale up if you're cooking for more.

Serves: 1
Prep: 10 minutes
Cook: 30 minutes

100g linguine, spaghetti or ziti
150g Tenderstem or ordinary
   broccoli, chopped
2 big handfuls of spinach
1 free-range egg, lightly beaten
2 heaped tablespoons
   crème fraîche
1/2 teaspoon chilli flakes
1 lemon, zest and juice
Sea salt, to taste
1 large salmon fillet
A big handful of panko
   or fresh white breadcrumbs
A big handful of grated Parmesan
A drizzle of olive oil

Preheat the oven to 180°C fan/200°C/gas 6. Bring a large pan of salted water to the boil, and cook the pasta for 10 minutes or according to the packet instructions. Add the broccoli to the pan for the last 2 minutes, and the spinach in the last 30 seconds. Drain well, reserving a small cup of cooking water.

Stir through the egg, crème fraîche, chilli flakes, lemon zest and juice, and as much of the pasta water as you need to get a nice saucy coating consistency. Taste, and add sea salt as needed.

Tip the pasta into a small roasting tin and lay the salmon fillet over the top, then scatter the breadcrumbs and Parmesan all over the salmon and pasta. Drizzle with a little oil to help the topping crisp up, and bake for 20 minutes, until the salmon is just cooked through, and the topping is golden. Serve immediately.

Note: You'll need to use a fairly thick salmon fillet if you prefer your salmon a little less cooked in the middle – I like the topping very crispy and don't mind the salmon a little more cooked, but you can adjust your cooking time as you prefer.

BARBECUE-STYLE RIBS WITH NEW POTATOES, SOUR CREAM & CHIVES

This is such an easy dish to feed a crowd, and scales up easily. The potatoes take on the most incredible flavour from cooking alongside the ribs in the barbecue marinade, and all you need to go alongside is a crisp green salad, and something cold to drink.

Serves: 4
Prep: 15 minutes
Cook: 1 hour 30 minutes

500g new potatoes
   (use Charlotte or a good
   roasting variety), halved
1kg free-range pork ribs
1 tablespoon olive oil
1 tablespoon Dijon mustard
1 tablespoon soy sauce
2 tablespoons
   Worcestershire sauce
1 tablespoon tomato purée
2 teaspoons smoked paprika
2 spring onions, thinly sliced
1 lime, juice and zest
120g sour cream or natural yogurt
Chives, thinly sliced

TO SERVE
Crisp green salad or coleslaw

Note: I've been known to pile the cooked ribs on a platter, make the dressing in a large bowl, and toss the roasted potatoes and the sticky in-the-tin leftover marinade directly into the sour cream dressing for a really spectacularly good potato salad to serve alongside.

Preheat the oven to 170°C fan/190°C/gas 5.

Tip the potatoes and ribs into a roasting tin or a lidded casserole dish large enough to hold the potatoes all in one layer. Mix together the olive oil, mustard, soy sauce, Worcestershire sauce, tomato purée and smoked paprika, work it into the ribs, then arrange them over the potatoes.

Pour in 400ml of water (on to the potatoes, rather than on to the rib marinade), then cover the dish tightly with foil or a lid, transfer to the oven and cook for 1 hour.

Meanwhile, mix together the spring onions, lime juice and zest and sour cream or yogurt, taste and adjust for salt and set aside.

After an hour, remove the foil, turn the oven up to 200°C fan/220°C/gas 7, and cook for a further 30 minutes, until the ribs are lovely and sticky and charred, and the cooking liquid has reduced.

Scatter everything with the chives, and serve the ribs and potatoes with the sour cream dip alongside and a crisp green salad or coleslaw.

S'MORES ROCKY ROAD WITH PEANUTS, MARSHMALLOWS & CHOCOLATE

This is possibly my proudest creation: chocolate refrigerator cake, or tiffin, crossed with rocky road, crossed with s'mores – the American campfire classic of Graham crackers and marshmallows sandwiched with a piece of chocolate, and toasted over a fire. In this version, the marshmallows just start to catch and caramelise under a hot oven. Perfect to take over to friends' houses, as it is rich and generously proportioned.

Serves: many, many people
Prep: 10 minutes
Cook: 10 minutes,
plus 1 hour chilling

200g unsalted butter
300g dark chocolate (minimum 70% cocoa solids, broken up
250g digestive biscuits or Graham crackers
150g mini vegetarian marshmallows (I like pink and white)
75g salted peanuts, roughly chopped

Preheat the oven to 180°C fan/200°C/gas 6. Tip the butter and chocolate into a saucepan over a low heat and stir until both have fully melted.

Break up all but 4 of the digestive biscuits or Graham crackers and stir them into the chocolate butter, then stir in 100g of the marshmallows. Spread the mixture in a lined shallow roasting tin, then scatter with the remaining digestive biscuits, broken into larger pieces, the marshmallows and the peanuts.

Transfer the tin to the oven and bake for 5–10 minutes, until the marshmallows have just started to catch and turn golden brown. Let the tin cool on the side before cutting the cake into squares. (I rather like a square or two while it's still warm out of the oven, but for a proper refrigerator cake, you'll need to pop it into the fridge to chill for a few hours before serving, so it sets properly.)

ASIA

RECIPES INSPIRED BY

THE INDIAN SUBCONTINENT,

CHINA & JAPAN

ASIA

TANDOORI CHICKEN WITH ROASTED SWEET POTATO
& MINT

BENGALI MUSTARD FISH WITH CAULIFLOWER & PEAS

SLOW-COOKED JACKFRUIT CURRY
WITH TAMARIND & COCONUT (VEGAN)

FESTIVAL LAMB, SPICED ROAST POTATOES,
PEAS & MINT RAITA

ALL-IN-ONE PILAU RICE WITH MUSHROOMS & SAFFRON (V)

KOREAN BARBECUE-STYLE CHICKEN, PEPPERS,
CARROTS & SPINACH

SPICED PANEER WITH POTATOES, PEAS & TOMATO (V)

LIME & COCONUT DAL (VEGAN)

SICHUAN CHICKEN, ROASTED SQUASH & GREENS

WHOLE BUTTER CHICKEN WITH SWEET POTATOES & RED ONION

KOREAN-STYLE AUBERGINES WITH SPRING ONIONS
& SESAME RICE (VEGAN)

LAMB KEEMA MEATBALLS, LEMON RICE, PEAS & MINT

MISO CHICKEN WITH AUBERGINES, SPRING ONIONS & CHILLI

INDIAN RICE PUDDING (V)

TANDOORI CHICKEN
WITH ROASTED SWEET POTATO & MINT

As a child, I ate vast quantities of this at Indian restaurants or at friends' barbecues, and have tried to come up with my own version ever since. It isn't the lurid red that I remember, as that's almost always food colouring, but you'll get a lovely colour and flavour from smoked paprika.

Serves: 4
Prep: 10 minutes
Cook: 1 hour

8 free-range chicken thighs,
  or thighs and drumsticks
2 large sweet potatoes, peeled
  and cut into 1 1/2 cm chunks
1 red onion, cut into eighths
6 tablespoons natural yogurt
1 tablespoon sunflower or olive oil
1 large lemon, zest and juice
5 cloves of garlic, grated
5cm ginger, grated
2 heaped teaspoons
  ground cumin
1 teaspoon ground turmeric
1 teaspoon mild chilli powder
1 1/2 teaspoons sea salt flakes
Freshly ground black pepper
4 heaped teaspoons smoked
  paprika
2 teaspoons garam masala

TO SERVE
200g natural yogurt
Cucumber, red onion,
  diced mango, fresh mint
Chapattis or naan bread

Preheat the oven to 180°C fan/200°C/gas 6.

Tip the chicken, sweet potatoes and red onion into a roasting tin large enough to hold everything in one layer. Mix together the yogurt, oil, lemon zest and juice, garlic, ginger, cumin, turmeric, chilli powder, salt, pepper and 2 heaped teaspoons of smoked paprika, and spread this evenly over the chicken, sweet potatoes and red onion, mixing to get everything well coated.

Scatter the chicken with the garam masala and another 2 teaspoons of smoked paprika, then transfer to the oven and roast for 1 hour.

Meanwhile, mix the yogurt with your choice of thinly sliced cucumber, red onion, mango or just a generous handful of fresh mint, taste and season with salt as needed, and set aside.

Let the chicken rest for 5–10 minutes before serving hot with the mint raita and chapattis or naan bread.

BENGALI MUSTARD FISH
WITH CAULIFLOWER & PEAS

Mustard and fish are a loved combination in Bengal. If you can get hold of Bengali mustard, kasundi, at your local Asian grocery store, this will be even nicer (and then you can use the rest of the bottle on everything from steak to spinach), but wholegrain mustard is a good substitute otherwise. The lightly spiced vegetables make this a meal in itself, but you can serve it with rice for extra carbs.

Serves: 4
Prep: 10 minutes
Cook: 25 minutes

1 cauliflower, cut into small florets
Cauliflower greens,
  cut into bite-size pieces
250g cherry tomatoes on the vine
200g frozen peas
1 red onion, thinly sliced
1/2 teaspoon ground turmeric
1 teaspoon ground cumin
1 teaspoon ground coriander
1 teaspoon sea salt flakes
2 tablespoons oil
4 nice thick cod fillets
4 teaspoons Bengali
  or wholegrain mustard

TO SERVE
Natural yogurt and basmati rice

Preheat the oven to 180°C fan/200°C Gas 6.

Tip the cauliflower, greens, cherry tomatoes, onion and peas into a roasting tin large enough to hold everything in one layer, and mix well with the spices, salt and oil.

Arrange the fish fillets over the vegetables, spread them with a teaspoon of mustard each, then transfer the tin to the oven and roast for 25 minutes, or until the fish is just cooked through.

Serve hot, with yogurt and rice alongside.

SLOW-COOKED JACKFRUIT CURRY WITH TAMARIND & COCONUT

This dish is very similar in taste to a classic South Indian *avial,* a delicious dish of vegetables with fresh coconut. The jackfruit works beautifully here with the coconut milk and tamarind, with added crunch from the carrots and beans.

Serves: 4
Prep: 10 minutes
Cook: 2 hours

2 x 600g tins of young jackfruit, drained (300g per tin drained weight)
1 onion, finely chopped
2 carrots, cut diagonally into 1cm half-moons
1 teaspoon ground coriander
1/2 teaspoon ground turmeric
1 fresh red chilli, pierced
2 cloves of garlic, grated
1 teaspoon sea salt flakes
1 x 400ml tin of coconut milk
4 heaped teaspoons tamarind paste
200–300g green beans, topped and tailed and cut into bite-size pieces
1 tablespoon coconut or sunflower oil
2 tablespoons vegan or natural yogurt

TO SERVE
Freshly cooked basmati rice or naan bread

Preheat the oven to 150°C fan/170°C/gas 3.

Tip the drained jackfruit, onion, carrots, spices, chilli, garlic, salt, coconut milk and tamarind paste into a lidded casserole dish or roasting tin. Cover with a lid or tightly with foil, then transfer to the oven for 1 1/2 hours.

After 1 1/2 hours, add the green beans, re-cover the dish or tin, then return it to the oven for a further 30 minutes.

As soon as the curry comes out of the oven, stir through the coconut or sunflower oil. Let it cool down for 5 minutes, then stir through the yogurt and serve hot with rice or naan bread.

FESTIVAL LAMB, SPICED ROAST POTATOES, PEAS & MINT RAITA

This is a dish that cannot fail to impress your guests – it looks wonderful brought to the table, but more importantly, the spicing on the lamb against the crisp potatoes and peas is completely moreish. If you're cooking for fewer than 6, you could definitely buy a half leg of lamb and halve the marinade quantities.

Serves: 4–6
Prep: 15 minutes
Cook: 3 hours

1.5kg Maris Piper or Desiree
    potatoes, cut into large
    6cm chunks
2 bay leaves
1 x 2kg leg of lamb
1 teaspoon fennel seeds
1 teaspoon ground ginger
1 teaspoon ground cumin
1 teaspoon chilli powder
1 teaspoon ground coriander
1 teaspoon sea salt flakes
6 green cardamom pods,
    seeds only
2 tablespoons olive oil
3 heaped tablespoons
    natural yogurt
200ml water
250g frozen peas

RAITA
250g natural yogurt
A handful of fresh mint,
    chopped
1 lime, juice only

Preheat the oven to 150°C fan/170°C/gas 3.

Tip the potatoes and bay leaves into a roasting tin large enough to hold them all in one layer, then lay the leg of lamb on top.

In a small bowl, mix together the fennel seeds, ginger, cumin, chilli, coriander, cardamom seeds, olive oil and yogurt. Rub the mixture all over the lamb – it's fine if some of it goes on the potatoes. Pour the water just over the potatoes, then cover the whole tin with foil, creating a good seal all around the edges. Transfer to the oven and cook for 2 hours and 15 minutes.

After the first stint, remove the foil, turn the oven up to 210°C fan/230°C/gas 8 and cook uncovered for 45 minutes, until the lamb and potatoes are crisp. Chuck the peas in for the final 5–10 minutes.

Let the lamb rest for 10–15 minutes, while you mix together the yogurt, mint and lime juice for the raita. Serve the raita alongside the lamb, peas and potatoes.

ALL-IN-ONE PILAU RICE
WITH MUSHROOMS & SAFFRON

Although I am something of a purist when it comes to pilau rice (the one my mother makes with cashew nuts is quite possibly the best thing I've ever eaten), this oven version with mushrooms is a new go-to – incredibly flavoursome for how little time it takes to put together. This dish will look beautiful with girolles or chanterelles if you can get them in season, but it's just as good year-round with chestnut mushrooms.

Serves: 4
Prep: 10 minutes
Cook: 30 minutes

3 big pinches of saffron
250g chestnut
  or wild mushrooms,
  whole if small,
  halved if large
200g basmati rice, rinsed
350ml vegetable stock
1 bay leaf
45g unsalted butter
100g unsalted cashew nuts
A handful of fresh coriander,
  chopped (optional)

TO SERVE
Natural yogurt

Note: I would say this is a meal in itself, because a bowl of rice certainly feels like one to me, but you could think about adding a fried egg or serving with a chickpea curry for a more traditionally balanced meal.

Preheat the oven to 210°C fan/230°C/gas 8.

While you're assembling your other ingredients, soak the saffron in a tablespoon of boiling water and let it steep for at least 5 minutes.

Tip the mushrooms, rice, stock, soaked saffron, bay leaf and 30g of the butter into a medium roasting tin or a lidded casserole dish. Cover very tightly with foil or the lid (this is important or the rice won't cook), then transfer to the oven and cook for 30 minutes.

When the rice has had 25 minutes, put the cashew nuts on a small baking tray with the remaining 15g butter and a pinch of sea salt, and pop the tray into the oven on another shelf.

Remove the rice and cashew nuts from the oven. Let the rice sit for a few minutes uncovered, taste and adjust the salt, then scatter over the nuts and coriander, if using, before serving with natural yogurt.

KOREAN BARBECUE-STYLE CHICKEN, PEPPERS, CARROTS & SPINACH

This is one of the most popular dishes in the book among my friends, and for good reason – once you have the ingredients, it's likely to become a weekly staple. If you haven't cooked Korean food before, don't be intimidated by the Korean red pepper paste (gochujang) – it's available in big branches of Sainsbury's and Asda at the time of writing. For Korean fermented soybean paste (doenjang), which is like miso paste's assertive cousin, you'll need to go online or to your nearest specialist supermarket, or use ordinary miso instead.

Serves: 4
Prep: 15 minutes
Cook: 1 hour

3 carrots, thickly sliced
2 red peppers, thickly sliced
125g shiitake mushrooms, whole
3 tablespoons sesame oil
2 teaspoons gochujang (Korean red pepper paste)
1 heaped teaspoon doenjang (Korean fermented soybean paste) or miso paste
1kg free-range chicken thighs and drumsticks (2 per person)
3–4 big handfuls of fresh spinach leaves

TO SERVE
Freshly cooked white rice

Preheat the oven to 170°C fan/190°C/gas 5.

Tip the carrots, peppers, shiitake mushrooms and 1 tablespoon of sesame oil into a roasting tin big enough to hold everything in one layer.

In a large bowl, mix the remaining 2 tablespoons of sesame oil, the gochujang and the doenjang or miso, then drop in the chicken pieces and coat thoroughly. Lay them over the vegetables, then transfer the tin to the oven and roast for 1 hour, until the skin is burnished and crispy and the chicken is cooked through.

Take the tin out of the oven and immediately add the spinach leaves, squashing them around the vegetables with a wooden spoon until they wilt. Let the chicken rest for 5–10 minutes, then serve hot with freshly cooked white rice.

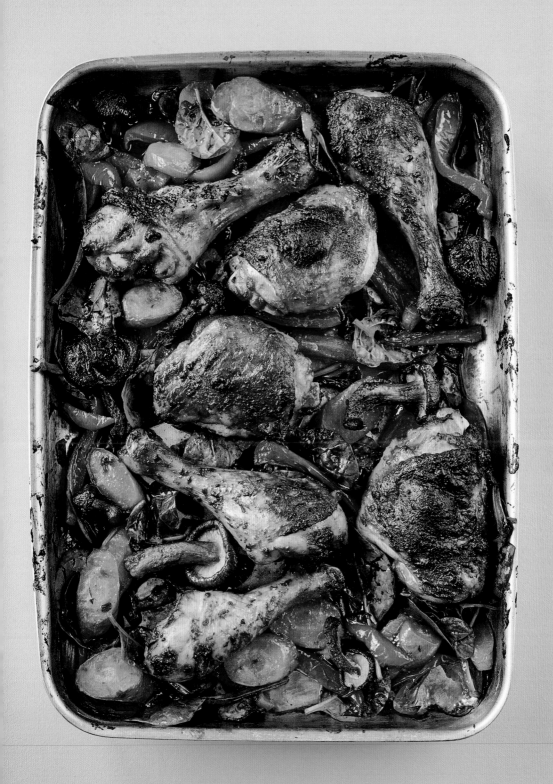

SPICED PANEER WITH POTATOES, PEAS & TOMATO

In the spirit of hope, this is one of my favourite dishes to order at an Indian restaurant – and while what arrives is always delicious, I inevitably rail against the ratio of paneer to potatoes. Cue the at-home oven version, with a generous amount of lightly spiced paneer to potatoes, fresh cherry tomatoes and just-cooked peas. One of my proudest creations.

Serves: 4
Prep: 15 minutes
Cook: 45 minutes

500g potatoes, cut into 1cm cubes
200g cherry tomatoes, halved
1 onion, roughly chopped
500g shop-bought paneer,
   cut into 2cm cubes
2 cloves of garlic, finely grated
5cm ginger, finely grated
2 tablespoons oil
½ teaspoon ground turmeric
1 teaspoon ground cumin
1 teaspoon ground coriander
1 teaspoon sea salt flakes
100ml water
250g frozen peas
1 lime, juice only

TO SERVE
Fresh coriander
Naan breads or rice

Preheat the oven to 180°C fan/200°C/gas 6.

Mix the potatoes, tomatoes, onion and paneer with the garlic, ginger, oil, spices and salt in a roasting tin large enough to hold everything in one layer, then transfer to the oven and roast for 35–40 minutes, until the paneer and potatoes are evenly browned and the potatoes are cooked through.

Tip in the water and peas and return the tin to the oven for a further 5–10 minutes, just to cook the peas through. Taste and season as needed with the lime juice and extra salt, then scatter with fresh coriander and serve with naan breads or white rice.

LIME & COCONUT DAL

This dal is based on one that my mother makes, with fresh coconut chunks and bright yellow channa dal. Channa dal has an exceptionally nice texture and flavour, but requires soaking and a long stint in the pan, so this version substitutes the quicker-cooking Egyptian red lentils. Roopa Gulati, another honorary food-mum, introduced me to the lime element – I can hands down say this is my favourite dal.

Serves: 2
Prep: 10 minutes
Cook: 45 minutes

140g red lentils, rinsed
1 scant teaspoon
    ground turmeric
1 x 400ml tin of coconut milk
90g fresh coconut pieces,
    cut into 1cm cubes
200ml boiling water
1 clove of garlic, unpeeled
1 onion, thinly sliced
1 teaspoon ground cumin
1 tablespoon oil
3–4 big handfuls of baby
    leaf spinach
2 limes, juice and zest
Sea salt flakes, to taste

TO SERVE
Freshly cooked rice,
    naan bread or chapattis
Lime wedges

Preheat the oven to 180°C fan/200°C/gas 6.

Tip the lentils, turmeric, coconut milk, coconut pieces, boiling water and garlic into a small roasting tin or lidded casserole dish. Mix the sliced onions, cumin and oil on your chopping board, then scatter them over the lentils. Cover tightly with foil or a lid, then transfer to the oven and cook for 45 minutes.

As soon as the dal is cooked, stir through the baby leaf spinach until it has just wilted. (I forgot to do this for the photograph opposite and accidentally put coriander on top, but don't let that stop you.) Adjust the texture to your preferred consistency with a little boiling water. Stir in the lime juice and zest, taste and adjust the salt, and serve with rice, naan bread or chapattis and extra lime wedges for squeezing.

Note: You can find fresh coconut pieces in little packets in the chiller cabinet at the supermarket, next to the cut-up pineapple and melon, which I find easier than chopping up a whole coconut for such a small quantity.

SICHUAN CHICKEN, ROASTED SQUASH & GREENS

Sichuan peppercorns are one of my favourite kitchen staples – stir-fried through hot rice, in a marinade for roast pork – and here, they work beautifully with chicken, squash, chilli and honey for a sweet and spicy traybake. Don't overdo the Sichuan peppercorns – they're mouth-numbing in large quantities, but if you're a fan of chilli, by all means increase the amount – Sichuan chicken is traditionally very spicy.

Serves: 2–3
Prep: 10 minutes
Cook: 45 minutes

3 teaspoons Sichuan peppercorns
1 1/2 teaspoons chilli flakes
   (less or more as needed)
600g butternut squash,
   cut into thin 1cm wedges
600g free-range, skinless,
   boneless chicken thighs
3 cloves of garlic, finely chopped
2 tablespoons sesame oil
1 tablespoon soy sauce
1 tablespoon honey
2 big pinches of sea salt flakes
200g pak choi, quartered

DRESSING
1 tablespoon soy sauce
1 tablespoon rice vinegar
1/2 tablespoon sesame oil

Preheat your oven to 180°C fan/200°C/gas 6.

Tip the Sichuan peppercorns and chilli flakes into a pestle and mortar, then coarsely pound them together for 30 seconds or so – you just want to break up the larger peppercorns.

Pop the squash, chicken, garlic, sesame oil, soy sauce and honey, along with the ground spices, into a roasting tin large enough to hold everything in one layer, and mix well so that everything is evenly coated. Scatter over the sea salt flakes, then transfer to the oven and roast for 30 minutes.

Remove the tin from the oven, scatter over the pak choi, then return to the oven and cook for a further 15 minutes.

Meanwhile, whisk the soy sauce, rice vinegar and sesame oil together. Spoon the dressing over the cooked chicken, pak choi and squash as soon as they come out of the oven, and serve hot.

Note: If you are a fan of chicken wings, this dish can easily be adapted wings instead of thighs.

WHOLE BUTTER CHICKEN
WITH SWEET POTATOES & RED ONION

This is a really celebratory roast chicken, with a completely addictive tomato sauce which cooks away happily underneath the tandoori-spiced bird. You may want to save it for a special occasion on account of the butter and cream – I think it's nice enough to have for a family dinner every few weeks or so.

Serves: 4
Prep: 15 minutes
Cook: 1 hour 30 minutes

50g butter
1 cinnamon stick
5 green cardamom pods, bashed
5 cloves
10cm ginger, grated
4 cloves of garlic, grated
3 large sweet potatoes, peeled
   and cut into large 5cm chunks
2 red onions, quartered
500g cherry tomatoes,
   with their vines
1 x 1.5kg free-range chicken
1 lime, zest and juice
2 teaspoons smoked paprika
1 teaspoon ground turmeric
2 teaspoons ground cumin
4 heaped tablespoons yogurt
1 tablespoon sunflower or olive oil
1 teaspoon sea salt flakes
150ml double cream

TO SERVE
Lime juice and sea salt flakes,
   to taste
Fresh coriander, roughly chopped

Preheat the oven to 180°C fan/200°C/gas 6.

Tip the butter, cinnamon stick, cardamom pods, cloves, half the grated ginger and garlic into a large roasting tin and pop it into the oven for 3–5 minutes to let the butter melt and the spices toast. Stir in the sweet potatoes, red onions and cherry tomatoes, along with their vines, and place the chicken on top.

Mix together the lime zest and juice and smoked paprika, turmeric, cumin, yogurt, oil, salt and the remaining ginger and garlic and slather this all over the chicken. Transfer to the oven and cook for 1 hour and 15 minutes.

Take the tin out of the oven, remove the vines, and squash down the cherry tomatoes with a wooden spoon. Stir in the double cream, then return it to the oven for a further 10 minutes, until the chicken is cooked through (it should read 70°C at the thickest part of the leg, not touching the bone if you use a meat thermometer).

Taste the sauce, and adjust the salt and lime juice as needed. Let the chicken rest for 10 minutes, then serve, scattered with fresh coriander.

KOREAN-STYLE AUBERGINES
WITH SPRING ONIONS & SESAME RICE

In the traditional Korean dish, aubergines are steamed for just 7 minutes before you gently stir in the red pepper and sesame dressing. In this version, I let the oven steam the aubergines, while fresh basmati rice and cabbage cook underneath for a simple and filling all-in-one dish. Gochugaru, or Korean red pepper flakes, are easily available online, at specialist shops, and even miraculously on Amazon – they really make the dish, and once you have a jar, you'll find yourself scattering the flakes on everything (scrambled eggs are my favourite).

Serves: 4
Prep: 15 minutes
Cook: 30 minutes

200g basmati rice, rinsed
2 cloves of garlic, unpeeled
2 leeks, or 1 small Chinese
   cabbage, thinly sliced
400ml vegetable stock
1 tablespoon sesame oil
2 aubergines, cut
   into 1 ½ cm slices
1 teaspoon sea salt flakes
3 fat spring onions,
   very thinly sliced
1 tablespoon sesame seeds

DRESSING
15g Korean red pepper flakes
   (gochugaru)
30ml sesame oil
30ml rice vinegar
30ml soy sauce
5cm ginger, grated
1 clove of garlic, finely grated

Preheat the oven to 210°C fan/230°C/gas 8.

Tip the rice and garlic into a wide lidded casserole dish or a medium roasting tin, then evenly cover with the sliced leeks or Chinese cabbage. Pour over the vegetable stock and sesame oil, then lay the aubergines over the top in one layer. Scatter over the sea salt, cover with the lid or very tightly with foil (this is important or the rice won't cook properly), then transfer to the oven and bake for 30 minutes.

Meanwhile, mix the dressing ingredients together. As soon as you take the tin out of the oven, remove the lid or foil and dress the aubergines with the red pepper dressing. Scatter over the spring onions and sesame seeds and serve hot.

LAMB KEEMA MEATBALLS, LEMON RICE, PEAS & MINT

My grandmother gave me her recipe for lamb keema and this is my version but made into meatballs. They steam gently on top of the lemon rice but crisp up right at the end with the lid off. A perfect weeknight dish - and popular with children.

Serves: 4
Prep: 15 minutes
Cook: 35 minutes

MEATBALLS
1 onion, peeled and halved
2 cloves of garlic, peeled
5cm ginger, peeled
10g fresh mint, leaves only
1 teaspoon ground coriander
2 teaspoons ground cumin
1 teaspoon fennel seeds
$1/2$ teaspoon ground turmeric
$1/2$ teaspoon chilli flakes
1 teaspoon salt
400g lamb mince
1 free-range egg

RICE
200g basmati rice, rinsed
400ml boiling chicken
  or lamb stock
$1/2$ lemon
200g chestnut mushrooms,
  halved
200g frozen peas
A couple of handfuls
  of flaked almonds

TO SERVE
10g fresh mint, leaves only
Natural yogurt

Preheat the oven to 210°C fan/230°C/gas 8.

Tip the onion, garlic, ginger, mint, spices and salt into a food processor and blitz until finely chopped. Tip in the lamb mince and egg and blitz again until fairly smooth. Alternatively, chop the onion, garlic, ginger and mint finely by hand and mix with the rest of the meatball ingredients.

Tip the rice and stock into a large shallow lidded casserole dish or roasting tin. squeeze in the lemon juice, then chop the skin into quarters and add to the rice. Scatter over the halved mushrooms and frozen peas.

With damp hands form the mince mixture into walnut-size balls, and dot them over the vegetables and rice. You should have about 20. Cover very tightly with foil (this is really important or the rice won't cook through) or the lid, then transfer to the oven and cook for 30 minutes.

After 30 minutes, remove the lid or foil, scatter over the flaked almonds, then return to the oven for a further 5 minutes. Scatter over the rest of the mint leaves and serve with yogurt alongside.

MISO CHICKEN
WITH AUBERGINES, SPRING ONIONS & CHILLI

This might be one of my favourite chicken dishes in the book, and it went through several versions before I arrived at this one, with just the right level of spice, miso, chilli and honey. I have been known to eat pieces of the chicken straight out of the tin, and if the pup is lucky, she gets tiny pieces of the chicken too.

Serves: 2
Prep: 10 minutes
Cook: 45 minutes

400g free-range boneless
  chicken thighs, halved
350g baby aubergines, halved
3 banana shallots, peeled
  and halved
2 1/2 cm ginger, grated
2 cloves of garlic, grated
2 tablespoons sesame oil
2 heaped tablespoons
  miso paste
1 tablespoon honey
1 teaspoon chilli flakes
1 tablespoon sesame seeds

DRESSING
1 lime, zest and juice
1 tablespoon sesame oil
1 tablespoon soy sauce

TO SERVE
3 spring onions, thinly sliced
Freshly cooked white rice

Preheat the oven to 180°C fan/200°C/gas 6.

Tip the chicken, aubergines and shallots into a roasting tin. Mix together the ginger, garlic, sesame oil, miso paste, honey, chilli flakes and sesame seeds in a small bowl, then evenly coat the chicken and aubergines with this mixture, making sure there's plenty on the top of each piece of chicken.

Transfer to the oven and roast for 45 minutes, until the chicken is golden brown and cooked through.

Mix the lime zest and juice, sesame oil and soy sauce and pour it all over the chicken and aubergine. Scatter over the spring onions, and serve hot, with rice on the side.

INDIAN RICE PUDDING

It's a tradition in both of my parents' families to make rice pudding for birthdays. In the South, where my father is from, it's a thinner version called *paysam*, with butter-fried cashew nuts to finish it off and plenty of cardamom, while my mother's favourite Calcutta version is thicker. I like my rice pudding thick enough to stand a spoon in, so this hybrid version has Indian spices and the all-important condensed milk, but the baked top you'd expect from a British rice pudding.

Serves: 6 (it's rich so you won't want too much)
Prep: 5 minutes
Cook: 1 hour

100g basmati rice, rinsed
800ml full-fat milk
1 x 400g tin of condensed milk
1 cinnamon stick
5 cardamom pods, bashed

TO SERVE
Slivered pistachio nuts (optional)

Preheat the oven to 180°C fan/200°C/gas 6.

Tip the rice, milk, condensed milk, cinnamon stick and cardamom pods into a small roasting tin or dish, cover tightly with foil, then transfer to the oven and bake for 50 minutes.

Remove the foil, then increase the heat to 200°C fan/220°C/gas 7 and return the tin to the oven for 5–10 minutes, until the top is just golden brown. Let the pudding cool down, then serve with pistachio nuts. In a rather leftfield way, I like a spoon of crème fraîche with this to cut through the richness.

AFRICA
& THE MIDDLE EAST

AFRICA & THE MIDDLE EAST

ROASTED CARROT, COURGETTE & BULGUR
WITH PISTACHIO & MINT (VEGAN)

CITRUS-SPIKED LAMB TAGINE
WITH APRICOTS & AUBERGINE

RAS-EL-HANOUT ROASTED COD
WITH CAULIFLOWER & POMEGRANATE

PERSIAN HERB FRITTATA (V)

PERI-PERI PRAWNS
WITH ROASTED SWEET POTATO & PEPPERS

BLACK-EYED BEANS
WITH TOMATOES, CHILLI & GINGER (VEGAN)

ZA'ATAR SPICED MEATBALLS WITH TOMATOES & BULGUR

CHERMOULA ROASTED TUNA, PEPPERS,
CHICKPEAS & RAISINS

ROASTED SQUASH, CRISPY LENTILS,
POMEGRANATE & DUKKAH (VEGAN)

SAFFRON PEARL BARLEY, RAINBOW VEGETABLES
& GREMOLATA (VEGAN)

ROASTED CAULIFLOWER & AUBERGINE
WITH FETA & ALMONDS (V)

PERSIAN LOVE CAKE WITH ROSE, CARDAMOM & FIGS

ROASTED CARROT, COURGETTE & BULGUR WITH PISTACHIO & MINT

This Middle Eastern inspired salad uses za'atar, a punchy mix of herbs and sesame seeds, as its flavouring. The sweetness of the dates and honey offsets the carrots and courgettes perfectly, with added richness from the pistachios at the end – you'd be hard pressed to notice that it's a vegan dish.

Serves: 2 as a main,
4 as a side
Prep: 15 minutes
Cook: 30 minutes

200g bulgur wheat
100g dates, halved
400ml vegetable stock
1 tablespoon olive oil
1 teaspoon sea salt
2 heaped tablespoons za'atar
150g baby carrots,
   halved lengthways
100g baby courgettes,
   halved lengthways
100g pistachios, roughly chopped
2 tablespoons extra virgin olive oil
1 lemon, zest and juice
1/2 tablespoon honey

TO SERVE
A big handful of fresh mint

Preheat the oven to 180°C fan/200°C/gas 6.

Tip the bulgur wheat, dates and stock into a medium roasting tin. Mix the olive oil, sea salt and za'atar with the halved baby carrots and courgettes on your chopping board, then scatter these evenly in one layer over the bulgur wheat. Transfer to the oven and bake for 30 minutes.

Meanwhile, mix the pistachios, extra virgin olive oil, lemon zest, juice and honey together and set aside.

Once cooked, scatter the pistachios and mint leaves all over the vegetables, and serve hot or at room temperature.

CITRUS-SPIKED LAMB TAGINE
WITH APRICOTS & AUBERGINE

When composing this recipe, I was curious to find out what a slow, gentle cook would do to nice ingredients in a tagine without browning them off first, and was delighted with the result – the aubergine and apricots work beautifully with the lamb and orange in this easy, oven-only version.

Serves: 4
Prep: 15 minutes
Cook: 2 hours 30 minutes

1 white onion, roughly chopped
5cm ginger, grated
2 plum tomatoes,
   roughly chopped
1 small aubergine,
   cut into 1 1/2 cm chunks
150–200g dried apricots
   (to taste: I like the sweetness
   of 200g, you may wish to start
   with 150g)
400g diced lamb
500ml boiling lamb or beef stock
3 heaped teaspoons ras-el-hanout
1 orange, zest and juice

TO SERVE
Hot cous cous
Fresh coriander, roughly chopped
Yogurt

Preheat the oven to 150°C fan/170°C/gas 3.

Tip all the ingredients into a roasting tin, lidded casserole dish or the bottom half of a tagine, stir, then cover tightly with foil or the lid. Transfer to the oven and cook for 2 hours and 30 minutes.

Just before the tagine is ready, make up the cous cous according to the packet instructions, and set aside. Serve the tagine hot, scattered with the fresh coriander, with the cous cous alongside and some yogurt if you wish.

Note: I have inauthentically suggested that you use ras-el-hanout as a quick-fix rather than a longer list of spices, because I like the full roundness of flavour that you get from it, but if you don't have any, use a teaspoon each of ground cumin and ground ginger, and 1/2 teaspoon each of ground cinnamon and paprika.

RAS-EL-HANOUT ROASTED COD
WITH CAULIFLOWER & POMEGRANATE

This is a real party piece of a dish – it looks stunning at the table, and packs in so much flavour for minimal prep time and effort. The chickpeas make the dish quite filling, but by all means add some extra carbs – my friend Laura likes to serve this with simply cooked lemony cous cous.

Serves: 4
Prep: 10 minutes
Cook: 25 minutes

1 large cauliflower,
  cut into small florets
  (along with the
  cauliflower greens)
1 red onion, thickly sliced
1 x 400g tin of chickpeas
2 teaspoons olive oil
2 tablespoons ras-el-hanout
1 teaspoon sea salt
4 thick cod fillets
Extra pinches of sea salt
  and ras el hanout

DRESSING
2 tablespoons extra virgin olive oil
1 lemon, zest and juice
1 teaspoon sea salt

TO SERVE
A generous handful
  of pomegranate seeds
Chopped fresh mint
Natural yogurt

Preheat the oven to 180°C fan/200°C/gas 6.

Tip the cauliflower, greens, onion and chickpeas into a roasting tin large enough to hold them and the cod fillets in one layer, then mix well with the olive oil, ras-el-hanout and sea salt.

Lay the cod fillets in the tin alongside the vegetables, and scatter each fillet with a little more sea salt and ras-el-hanout. Transfer to the oven and roast for 25 minutes.

Meanwhile, mix the extra virgin olive oil, lemon zest and juice, and sea salt together and set aside. Once the cod and cauliflower are cooked through, pour over the dressing, scatter over the pomegranate seeds and chopped mint, and serve with natural yogurt alongside.

PERSIAN HERB FRITTATA

I love Iranian food, and one of my favourite things about it is the incredible quantities of herbs which go into a recipe. Forget a little scatter of flat-leaf parsley to finish a dish – you add herbs to dishes like this classic Persian frittata by the handful, and they are all the better for it. Perfect at room temperature, or sliced and packed cold for picnics or packed lunches.

Serves: 2 as part of a main
            4 as a side/starter
Prep: 10 minutes
Cook: 25–30 minutes

50g flat-leaf parsley,
  finely chopped
20g fresh dill, finely chopped
Leaves from 10 sprigs
  of fresh mint, finely chopped
2 cloves of garlic, grated
1 teaspoon sea salt
30g plain flour
6 free-range eggs
50g hard goat's cheese, grated
3 spring onions, finely chopped
20g walnuts, finely chopped

Preheat the oven to 160°C fan/180°C/gas 4.

Whisk the herbs, garlic, salt, flour, eggs and all but a handful of the goat's cheese together, then pour into a small roasting tin or baking dish lined with non-stick baking parchment. You want the egg mixture to be about 1 inch deep in the tin.

Scatter over the remaining cheese, then transfer to the oven and bake for 25–30 minutes, until the top is just golden brown, and the egg is cooked through (a knife inserted into the middle should come out clean, not eggy).

Let the frittata cool for 10 minutes in the tin before turning it out on to a plate. Scatter over the spring onions and walnuts and serve warm, or at room temperature.

PERI-PERI PRAWNS
WITH ROASTED SWEET POTATO & PEPPERS

Popular in Mozambique, Angola and South Africa, peri-peri sauce combines chilli, garlic and paprika for dishes with a real kick. If you're a chilli fiend, try to get hold of African bird's-eye chillies – I use milder ones for personal preference, but this is a lovely dish that you can customise to taste.

Serves: 2
Prep: 10 minutes
Cook: 40 minutes

350g slim sweet potatoes,
   cut into 1cm rounds
2 red peppers, thinly sliced
1 red onion, thinly sliced
1 tablespoon softened butter
2 tablespoons olive oil
4 cloves of garlic, grated
2 teaspoons paprika
2 hot red chillies, very finely
   chopped (more or less
   as you wish)
1 tablespoon red wine vinegar
   or lemon juice
1 teaspoon sea salt
250g raw king prawns
1/2 lemon, juice only

TO SERVE
Lemon wedges and sour cream

Preheat the oven to 180°C fan/200°C/gas 6.

Tip the sweet potatoes, peppers and onion into a roasting tin large enough to hold everything in one layer. Mix the softened butter, olive oil, garlic, paprika, chillies, vinegar or lemon juice and salt together in a bowl, then tip all but 1 tablespoon of this over the vegetables. Mix well, then transfer to the oven and roast for 35 minutes.

Mix the remaining tablespoon of the peri-peri mix with the prawns as a marinade, and set aside in the fridge.

After 35 minutes, scatter the prawns over the vegetables and return the tin to the oven for a further 8–10 minutes, until the prawns are pink and cooked through.

Squeeze over the lemon juice, taste the prawns and veg and adjust the salt to taste, then serve with lemon wedges and sour cream.

BLACK-EYED BEANS
WITH TOMATOES, CHILLI & GINGER

Galvin cooked at the house I stayed at in Kampala; she was inventive with her recipes, and her secret seemed to be to use more oil in a dish than we'd ever seen before (her pasta sauce was pretty much 50:50 tomatoes and peppers to olive oil, and delicious for it). I was delighted to find when researching this Ugandan bean recipe that one version called for 500ml oil – it wasn't just her! But I've toned it down to 4 tablespoons here – this is a rich and filling dish.

Serves: 4
Prep: 10 minutes
Cook: 50 minutes

1 white onion, roughly chopped
2 red peppers, roughly chopped
2 cloves of garlic, grated
5cm ginger, grated
1 heaped teaspoon paprika
1 heaped teaspoon ground cumin
4 tablespoons olive oil
sea salt flakes
1 x 400g tin of black-eyed beans
  in water
1 x 400g tin of kidney beans
  in water
1 x 400g tin of tomatoes
3 spring onions, thinly sliced
1 Scotch bonnet pepper, pierced
lemon juice, to taste

TO SERVE
Thinly sliced spring onions
  and rice

Preheat the oven to 180°C fan/200°C/gas 6.

Tip the onion, peppers, garlic, ginger, spices, half the oil and 1 teaspoon of sea salt flakes into a roasting tin large enough to hold them all in roughly one layer, mix well, then transfer to the oven and roast for 20 minutes.

After 20 minutes, tip in the beans, along with their liquid, the tinned tomatoes, remaining olive oil and spring onions. Stir, pop the Scotch bonnet into the liquid, then return to the oven for 30 minutes.

Once cooked, taste and add more salt and a squeeze of lemon juice as needed. Don't worry if the sauce looks a little thin – it will thicken as it sits. Remove the Scotch bonnet, scatter over the spring onions and serve with rice alongside.

NOTE: You can use just black-eyed beans if you like, but I like a mixture of black-eyed and kidney.

ZA'ATAR SPICED MEATBALLS
WITH TOMATOES & BULGUR

These simply spiced meatballs with parsley and feta work beautifully cooked with bulgur wheat and tomatoes for a really lovely all-in-one meal. I like making the meatballs fairly small, to sit on top of the bulgur – you need nothing more than a little natural yogurt alongside to serve.

Serves: 4
Prep: 15 minutes
Cook: 25 minutes

400g lamb mince
50g flat-leaf parsley,
   leaves and stalks
1 free-range egg
100g feta cheese
4 teaspoons za'atar
1 teaspoon sea salt flakes
200g bulgur wheat, rinsed
250g vine cherry tomatoes,
   halved, with their vines
1 red onion, thinly sliced
400ml chicken stock
1 tablespoon olive oil
1 lemon, juice only

TO SERVE
A handful of fresh coriander,
   chopped
Natural yogurt

Preheat the oven to 180°C fan/200°C/gas 6.

Tip the lamb mince, parsley, egg, feta, za'atar and sea salt into a food processor, blitz until everything is evenly mixed, then set aside.

Tip the bulgur wheat and the cherry tomato vines into a large roasting tin, then top with the halved cherry tomatoes and the red onion. Pour over the chicken stock and olive oil, then, with damp hands, form the lamb mixture into small walnut-size meatballs (you should get around 26) and dot them over the bulgur.

Transfer the tin to the oven and bake for 25 minutes, until the meatballs are just browned and the bulgur is cooked through. Squeeze over the lemon juice, scatter with coriander and serve with natural yogurt alongside.

CHERMOULA ROASTED TUNA, PEPPERS, CHICKPEAS & RAISINS

Chermoula is a North African spice paste, the perfect marinade for fish and vegetables, and it's easy to make. Traditionally you'd use coriander, but I love using fresh mint. I'd happily eat this at a restaurant: a wonderful combination of flavours and textures.

Serves: 4
Prep: 15 minutes
Cook: 50 minutes

CHERMOULA
45g fresh mint, leaves only
1 ½ teaspoons ground cumin
1 ½ teaspoons ground paprika
4 cloves of garlic, peeled
3 tablespoons olive oil
A pinch of sea salt
1 preserved lemon
   or ½ lemon, zest only,
   and 1 teaspoon white vinegar

3 colourful pointy peppers,
   halved
1 medium aubergine,
   cut into eighths
1 red onion, cut into 1cm slices
300g cherry tomatoes,
   with their vines
1 x 400g tin of chickpeas, drained
4 nice thick tuna steaks
100g raisins
100ml warm water
A handful of flaked almonds

TO SERVE
A handful of fresh mint

Preheat the oven to 180°C fan/200°C/gas 6.

Tip all the chermoula ingredients into a blender and blitz until combined. Taste and add a little more salt as needed.

Tip the peppers, aubergine, onion, cherry tomatoes with their vines and the chickpeas into a roasting tin large enough to more or less hold the vegetables in one layer. Mix through three-quarters of the chermoula, making sure to coat the vegetables evenly, then transfer to the oven and roast for 40 minutes.

Meanwhile, spread the remaining chermoula all over the tuna steaks, then return them to the fridge to marinate. Don't wash the blender – tip in the raisins and water, stir and set aside.

Once the vegetables have had 40 minutes, tip in the raisins and liquid. Remove the tomato vines, squash down the tomatoes, then lay the tuna over the vegetables. Scatter over the almonds, then return to the oven for 10–12 minutes, until the tuna is just cooked and the almonds are crisp.

Scatter over the mint and serve.

ROASTED SQUASH, CRISPY LENTILS, POMEGRANATE & DUKKAH

If you enjoy making Middle Eastern or Ottolenghi recipes, you'll probably have a bottle of pomegranate molasses and a jar of dukkah stashed in your cupboard – this dish is the perfect opportunity to use them. I like to add the dukkah at the end, as it can burn in the oven on a high heat – it adds wonderful crunch and flavour to the roasted vegetables and lentils.

Serves: 4
Prep: 15 minutes
Cook: 45–50 minutes

600g squash,
  cut into 1 1/2 cm slices
1 red onion, cut into eighths
250g cherry tomatoes,
  on the vine
1 x 400g tin of brown lentils,
  drained and rinsed
1 teaspoon sea salt
2 tablespoons pomegranate
  molasses
2 tablespoons olive oil
3 cloves of garlic, grated
1 teaspoon chilli flakes
  (less if yours are very hot)
2 tablespoons dukkah
A handful of pomegranate seeds
A handful of fresh dill or mint,
  roughly chopped

DRESSING
100ml vegan yogurt
2 tablespoons pomegranate
  molasses

Preheat the oven to 180°C fan/200°C/gas 6.

Tip the squash, onion and tomatoes into a roasting tin large enough to hold everything in one layer, then mix through the lentils, salt, pomegranate molasses, oil, garlic and chilli flakes. Transfer to the oven and roast for 45–50 minutes, until the squash is cooked through.

Meanwhile, mix the vegan yogurt and pomegranate molasses together, then taste and season as needed with a pinch of salt. Drizzle the yogurt over the roasted veg, scatter over the dukkah, pomegranate seeds and mint and serve hot.

SAFFRON PEARL BARLEY, RAINBOW VEGETABLES & GREMOLATA

One of my friends meticulously cuts up mountains of vegetables for soup every other week or so and this dish is inspired by his recipe. I like the addition of a good amount of pearl barley, so this thick soupy-stew is a meal in itself. The gremolata-style mixture of garlic, lemon zest and parsley to finish really makes this dish – reserve a spoonful to put on each bowl just before serving.

Serves: 4–6 (good for lunchboxes)
Prep: 15 minutes
Cook: 1 hour

4 big pinches of good saffron
  (I like Belazu)
900ml vegetable stock
200g pearl barley, rinsed
2 leeks, thinly sliced
1 small head of fennel,
  thinly sliced
2 red peppers, roughly chopped
1 small carrot, roughly chopped
1 x 400g tin of chickpeas, drained
Sea salt flakes, to taste

DRESSING
2 small cloves of garlic,
  finely chopped
1 lemon, zest and juice
30ml olive oil
20g flat-leaf parsley,
  finely chopped

Preheat the oven to 180°C fan/200°C/gas 6.

Tip the saffron, vegetable stock and pearl barley into a deep roasting tin or lidded casserole dish and top with the leeks, fennel, peppers, carrot and chickpeas. Cover with foil or the lid, then transfer to the oven and cook for 1 hour.

Meanwhile, mix the garlic, lemon zest and juice, olive oil and parsley and set aside.

Once cooked, taste the pearl barley and vegetables and adjust the salt as needed. If serving immediately, stir through the oil and parsley dressing, taste and adjust the lemon and salt as needed and serve. If you aren't serving it all immediately, serve with a dollop of the parsley dressing on each bowl.

NOTE: If you don't have the time or inclination to make the gremolata dressing or you're having leftovers the next day, you can substitute good bought vegan pesto from the supermarket chilled cabinet – I have definitely done this when I've been in a hurry and it works beautifully.

ROASTED CAULIFLOWER & AUBERGINE WITH FETA & ALMONDS

This is a nice simple veg-filled traybake, with a good contrast of textures and flavours: crisp, spiced cauliflower, soft feta, crunch from the almonds and a herby, lemony dressing. I've served it as a dinner party starter, but it would work just as well with flatbreads or cous cous for an easy weeknight dinner.

Serves: 4
Prep: 10 minutes
Cook: 40 minutes

2 aubergines,
   cut into thin wedges
1 cauliflower, cut into small florets
Cauliflower greens,
   cut into bite-size pieces
   (young leaves only)
1 red onion, cut into eighths
2 tablespoons olive oil
1 heaped teaspoon ground ginger
1 heaped teaspoon ground
   coriander
1 heaped teaspoon ground cumin
1 teaspoon sea salt flakes
A big handful of fresh coriander,
   roughly chopped
100g feta cheese, crumbled
50g flaked almonds, toasted

DRESSING
1 lemon, zest and juice
1 tablespoon extra virgin olive oil
1 teaspoon honey

TO SERVE
Natural yogurt and flatbreads
   or cous cous

Preheat the oven to 180°C fan/200°C/gas 6.

Tip the aubergine, cauliflower, cauliflower greens and onion into a roasting tin large enough to hold everything in one layer, then mix through the olive oil, ginger, ground coriander, cumin and sea salt, making sure to work it into the cauliflower florets.

Transfer to the oven and roast for 40 minutes, until the aubergine is just cooked through, and the cauliflower is nice and charred.

Mix the lemon zest and juice with the olive oil and honey and drizzle over the vegetables. Scatter over the fresh coriander, feta cheese and flaked almonds and serve with yogurt and flatbreads or cous cous alongside.

PERSIAN LOVE CAKE
WITH ROSE, CARDAMOM & FIGS

Like Scheherezade's tales, there are thousands of versions of Persian love cake, with the roughly similar legend behind them that a young woman made the cake for the man she loved, who promptly and helpfully fell in love with her on tasting it. I can make no guarantees as to the efficacy of this recipe for similar results, as the man was a prince and that was a fairytale, but nonetheless this is a lovely, baklava-scented cake to make for friends or loved ones.

Serves: 8
Prep: 15 minutes
Cook: 25 minutes

170g soft light brown sugar
170g soft unsalted butter
3 nice free-range eggs
125g self-raising flour
1 teaspoon baking powder
45g ground almonds
1/2 teaspoon ground cinnamon
4 cardamom pods, seeds only
2 drops of rosewater

ICING
250g mascarpone
25g icing sugar
1–2 drops of rosewater

DECORATION
Fresh edible or dried rose petals
   (optional)
A handful of pistachio slivers
2 fresh figs, thinly sliced

Preheat the oven to 160°C fan/180°C/gas 4. Beat the sugar and butter together until soft, then whisk in the eggs. Fold in the flour, baking powder, ground almonds, spices and rosewater, then transfer the mixture to a lined 26cm by 20cm shallow roasting tin and bake for 25–30 minutes, until the cake is golden brown and a skewer, when inserted, comes out clean.

Meanwhile, beat the mascarpone and icing sugar together with one or two tiny drops of rosewater (depending on the brand, it can be very strong so use it carefully).

Once the cake is out of the oven, let it cool for 5 minutes in the tin, then transfer to a wire rack until completely cold. Spread the icing all over the cake neatly with a hot palette knife, then scatter over the rose petals, pistachio slivers and quartered figs.

NOTE: This cake freezes well un-iced. If you are not eating it on the day you make it, store in the fridge as the topping uses fresh fruit.

SOUTH EAST ASIA & AUSTRALASIA

SOUTH EAST ASIA & AUSTRALASIA

THAI BEEF PANANG WITH COCONUT, CHILLI & PEANUTS

ROASTED AUBERGINE WITH PEANUTS,
CHILLI & LIME (VEGAN)

MALAYSIAN CHICKEN LAKSA
WITH BEANSPROUTS & NOODLES

MALAYSIAN ROAST CHICKEN WITH COCONUT,
LEMONGRASS & SQUASH

STEAK & ALE PIE WITH MUSHROOMS & ROSEMARY

BLACK PEPPER TOFU, CHOI SUM & CASHEWS (VEGAN)

PERANAKAN-STYLE MUSHROOM & SQUASH
KAPITAN CURRY (VEGAN)

INDONESIAN-STYLE AUBERGINE & POTATOES
WITH GARLIC & CHILLI (VEGAN)

INDONESIAN COCONUT RICE, CRISPY CHILLI TOFU
& PEANUT SAMBAL (VEGAN)

ROASTED SPICED MUSHROOMS & PANEER
WITH SQUASH, POMEGRANATE & MANGO (V)

HOT-SMOKED SALMON FRITTATA WITH YOGURT & DILL

FILIPINO-STYLE VEGETABLE ADOBO
WITH GARLIC & BAY (VEGAN)

SALTED CHOCOLATE & RASPBERRY LAMINGTONS (V)

THAI BEEF PANANG
WITH COCONUT, CHILLI & PEANUTS

This dish is a revelation: beef cooked in coconut with lemongrass and chilli, with a depth of flavour from shrimp paste and lime. I give two ways to make the panang paste, because if you are in a hurry, you can use a packet of Thai red curry paste and add extra ingredients to it, while the more authentic version is given in the note below.

Serves: 4
Prep: 15 minutes
Cook: 30 minutes

400g quick-cook stir-fry
   beef strips
100g Thai red curry paste
   (or see note below)
2 cardamom pods, seeds only
2 teaspoons ground coriander
1 teaspoon ground cumin
2 tablespoons salted peanuts,
   finely chopped
1 tablespoon soft brown sugar
1 x 400ml tin of coconut milk
2 red peppers, thickly sliced
1 x 180g packet of shiitake
   mushrooms

TO SERVE
A handful of fresh coriander
Sliced red chillies
A handful of chopped salted
   peanuts
Noodles or rice

Preheat the oven to 160°C fan/180°C/gas 4.

Tip the beef strips into a medium roasting tin or casserole dish (fairly shallow is good, as it allows the beef to brown). Mix the Thai red curry paste or your homemade paste (see below) with the cardamom, coriander, cumin, salted peanuts and brown sugar, rub this all over the beef, then transfer to the oven and cook for 10 minutes.

After 10 minutes, stir through the coconut milk, red peppers and mushrooms and mix everything so the beef sits on top of the vegetables. Return to the oven for 20 minutes.

Scatter over coriander leaves, chillies and peanuts and serve with noodles or rice.

Note: If you would like to make the panang paste from scratch rather than use bought Thai red curry paste, blitz together 2 shallots, 5cm of galangal, 2 cloves of garlic (all peeled), 1 red chilli, 4 kaffir lime leaves, 1 teaspoon of shrimp paste and 2 sticks of lemongrass. Add the dry spices to this as above.

ROASTED AUBERGINE
WITH PEANUTS, CHILLI & LIME

The peanut dressing for this quick and easy dish works so well with the aubergines and pepper – perfect to serve alongside rice or noodles. As brands of peanut butter vary, you may need to spend a little time beating it with the soy sauce and sesame oil to get a good spoonable consistency – but it's well worth it.

Serves: 2 generously
Prep: 15 minutes
Cook: 45 minutes

2 aubergines, cut lengthways
  into eighths
1 red pepper, roughly sliced
170g baby corn
3 cloves of garlic, grated
5cm ginger, grated
1 teaspoon sea salt flakes
2 tablespoons sesame oil
Lots of freshly ground
  black pepper

DRESSING
1 heaped tablespoon crunchy
  peanut butter (approx. 75g)
2 tablespoons good soy sauce
1 tablespoon sesame oil
4 tablespoons water
2–4 limes, juice only
1 fresh red chilli, thinly sliced

TO SERVE
A handful of fresh coriander,
  chopped
Quick-cook rice or noodles

Preheat the oven to 180°C fan/200°C/gas 6.

Tip the aubergines, red pepper and corn into a tin large enough to hold them all in one layer and mix through the garlic, ginger, salt, sesame oil and black pepper. Transfer to the oven and roast for 45 minutes.

Meanwhile, mix together all the ingredients for the dressing and set aside. (You want a good spoonable consistency, something like double cream, so you may need to add a little more water to adjust the texture depending on your brand of peanut butter).

Once the aubergines are cooked through, pour over the dressing, taste and adjust the salt as needed, scatter over the fresh coriander and serve hot with quick-cook rice or noodles.

MALAYSIAN CHICKEN LAKSA
WITH BEANSPROUTS & NOODLES

This laksa is intensely savoury, sharp and fully flavoured, and rounded off by the sweet coconut. You could also add a handful of cooked prawns along with the noodles and beansprouts, if you wish.

Serves: 4
Prep: 15 minutes
Cook: 45 minutes

2 x 400ml tins of coconut milk
600g free-range boneless
  chicken thighs, diced
2 sticks of lemongrass, bashed
20g fresh mint, leaves chopped
20g fresh coriander, chopped
200ml boiling fish stock
1 tablespoon light brown sugar
1 teaspoon sea salt flakes
225g fresh rice vermicelli noodles
  (from the chilled cabinet)
1 x 300g packet of beansprouts
1–2 limes, juice only

SPICE MIX
4 banana shallots, peeled
8cm ginger, peeled
5 cloves of garlic, peeled
3 fresh red chillies
40g shrimp paste
1 heaped teaspoon ground
  turmeric
2 heaped teaspoons ground
  coriander

TO SERVE
Lime wedges and sliced chilli

Preheat the oven to 180°C fan/200°C/gas 6.

Blitz the spice mix ingredients in a small blender or food processor (with a tablespoon of coconut milk if needed to loosen the mix). Tip the chicken into a shallow casserole dish or roasting tin, cover well with the spice mix, then transfer to the oven and roast for 15 minutes.

Add the lemongrass, two-thirds of the mint and coriander, the remaining coconut milk, the fish stock, sugar and salt, stir, then cover with a lid or foil and return the dish to the oven for a further 30 minutes.

Remove the laksa from the oven, add the noodles and beansprouts, then cover and leave for 5 minutes for them to soften through. Add the lime juice, then taste and adjust the salt, sugar and lime as needed. Scatter with the rest of the coriander and mint and serve with lime wedges and fresh chilli.

MALAYSIAN ROAST CHICKEN
WITH COCONUT, LEMONGRASS & SQUASH

This is my traybake version of the Malaysian classic ayam percik, or coconut roast chicken, and it will make your kitchen smell absolutely incredible. It's mild enough to give to children, but interesting enough to serve to adults with freshly chopped red chilli added to taste.

Serves: 4
Prep: 15 minutes
Cook: 1 hour

1 x 400ml tin of coconut milk
1kg free-range chicken thighs
  and drumsticks
600g butternut squash,
  thinly sliced
3 shallots, peeled and halved

SPICE PASTE
3 shallots, peeled
5cm ginger, peeled
4 cloves of garlic, peeled
1 red chilli, stem removed
1 teaspoon ground turmeric
2 teaspoons ground coriander
2 sticks of lemongrass
3 tablespoons tamarind paste
5 macadamia nuts (optional)
2 teaspoons brown sugar

TO SERVE
Thinly sliced chilli and chopped
  fresh coriander
Freshly cooked rice

Preheat the oven to 180°C fan/200°C/gas 6.

Tip all the ingredients for the spice paste into a food processor or a high-speed blender with enough of the coconut milk to make everything blend fairly smoothly together.

Mix the paste with the remaining coconut milk, then tip it into a roasting tin along with the chicken, squash and shallots, making sure there's plenty of the sauce over the chicken.

Transfer to the oven and roast for 1 hour, until the chicken is golden brown and cooked through and the squash is soft. Scatter over thinly sliced chilli and chopped coriander and serve with hot rice.

STEAK & ALE PIE
WITH MUSHROOMS & ROSEMARY

Steak and ale pie is an Australian classic. It's absolutely worth putting in the fifteen minutes prep to have this ridiculously nice pie, or a number of smaller ones in the fridge for the week. Use all-butter puff pastry if you can get it – it makes a subtle but noticeable difference.

Serves: 4
Prep: 15 minutes
Cook: 3 hours 30 minutes

700g beef braising steak, cubed
2 leeks, thinly sliced
2 carrots, halved and thickly sliced
450g chestnut mushrooms, halved
2 sprigs of fresh rosemary, needles finely chopped
400ml boiling beef stock
400ml pale ale (I like to use Neck Oil)
1 tablespoon Worcestershire sauce
Large quantities of freshly ground black pepper
1 heaped teaspoon cornflour
1 x 420g roll of puff pastry (if you can get all-butter, it'll be even nicer)
1 egg beaten

Preheat the oven to 150°C fan/170°C/gas 3.

Tip the steak, leeks, carrots, mushrooms and rosemary into a large lidded casserole dish or roasting tin, then pour over the stock, ale, and Worcestershire sauce. Season really liberally with pepper, then stir, cover with the lid or tightly with foil and transfer to the oven for 3 hours.

After 3 hours, remove the casserole dish or roasting tin from the oven and turn the heat up to 180°C fan/200°C/gas 6. Mix the cornflour with a tablespoon of cold water, then pour it into the dish, and stir. Carefully lay the puff pastry over the dish or roasting tin, crimping it over the edges, cut a hole or cross in the centre and brush with the beaten egg. Then return it to the oven for a further 30 minutes, until the pastry is crisp and golden brown.

Let the pie rest for 5 minutes, then serve, hot.

Note: If you would like to make smaller pies, buy 2 rolls of puff pastry. Tip the cooked filling evenly between 4 pie dishes, cut out 4 lids from the pasty, and proceed.

BLACK PEPPER TOFU, CHOI SUM & CASHEWS

This dish went through a few versions before I was completely happy, and now I could eat a trayful along with the very addictive dressing. Buy a good brand of firm tofu which will crisp up in the oven – it works beautifully with the simple black pepper, ginger and garlic seasoning.

Serves: 4
Prep: 15 minutes
Cook: 40 minutes

150g shiitake mushrooms
200g chestnut mushrooms
175g baby corn
2 x 280g packets of firm tofu,
   cut into 2cm cubes
2 tablespoons sesame oil
1 tablespoon freshly ground
   black pepper
2 teaspoons sea salt
2 cloves of garlic, grated
5cm ginger, grated
200g choi sum or pak choi,
   roughly chopped
50g cashew nuts

DRESSING
2 tablespoons sesame oil
1 lime, zest and juice
1 tablespoon soy sauce
1 tablespoon rice vinegar
1 teaspoon chilli flakes

TO SERVE
Quick-cook noodles or rice
Chives

Preheat the oven to 200°C fan/220°C/gas 7.

Tip the mushrooms (halved if large), baby corn and tofu into a roasting tin large enough to hold everything in one layer, then mix in the sesame oil, black pepper, sea salt, garlic and ginger. Grind a little extra black pepper just over the tofu pieces, then transfer to the oven and roast for 25 minutes.

Tip the chopped choi sum or pak choi and the cashew nuts into the roasting tin, then return it to the oven for a further 15 minutes, until the tofu is golden brown and the greens are wilted.

Meanwhile, mix together the sesame oil, lime zest and juice, soy sauce, rice vinegar and chilli flakes and pour over this dressing as soon as the dish comes out of the oven.

Scatter with chives and serve with quick-cook noodles or rice.

Note: My mother likes to use the Cauldron marinated tofu for extra flavour.

PERANAKAN-STYLE MUSHROOM & SQUASH KAPITAN CURRY

Every time I visit Singapore, I'm hosted by my friend Kristin, who makes it her mission to take me to the best places to eat during my stay. We decided that our favourite regional dishes – chilli crab, deep-fried bread, chilli wontons and char siu bao – might be a little difficult to recreate in a tin, but that one of the Peranakan or Nyonya dishes would work perfectly. This curry is usually made with chicken, but works beautifully with mushrooms and squash.

Serves: 4
Prep: 10 minutes
Cook: 45 minutes

250g portabellini or large
  chestnut mushrooms
150g shiitake mushrooms
500g butternut squash,
  cut into 1cm slices
2 shallots, roughly chopped
2 tablespoons sunflower
  or olive oil
320ml coconut cream
  or thick coconut milk
4 teaspoons tamarind paste
1 tablespoon galangal paste
  (or grated fresh galangal)
1 tablespoon soy sauce
2 sticks of lemongrass, broken
3 kaffir lime leaves
5cm ginger, grated
2 cloves of garlic, grated
1 teaspoon ground turmeric
1 teaspoon mild chilli powder

TO SERVE
Rice and chopped fresh coriander

Preheat the oven to 180°C fan/200°C/gas 6.

Tip the mushrooms and squash into a roasting tin large enough to hold them comfortably in one layer, then mix through all the remaining ingredients, making sure that the vegetables are evenly coated.

Transfer to the oven and cook for 45 minutes, until the squash is cooked through and the sauce has reduced.

Taste and adjust with salt or soy sauce as needed, scatter with fresh coriander, and serve with rice alongside.

VEGAN

INDONESIAN-STYLE AUBERGINES & POTATOES WITH GARLIC & CHILLI

This is my version of an Indonesian dish known as balado, a dish with a sauce made of chilli, tomatoes, garlic, shallots and lime juice. It works perfectly with aubergines and potatoes, and while it's usually stir-fried, it works beautifully in the oven as well. The spice level is pretty high for me given that I barely eat any chilli, but my friend and fellow food writer Ella Risberger assured me she could taste flavours other than chilli while I inhaled a pot of yogurt to counter the heat.

Serves: 4
Prep: 15 minutes
Cook: 45 minutes

3 shallots, peeled
4 cloves of garlic, peeled
2 fresh red chillies,
  stems removed
2 tablespoons sunflower
  or olive oil
1 tablespoon sugar
2 teaspoons sea salt flakes
250g cherry tomatoes on the vine
350g baby aubergines, halved
500g Charlotte potatoes, halved
  if small, quartered if large
1 lime, juice only

TO SERVE
A handful of fresh coriander,
  chopped
Freshly cooked white rice

Preheat the oven to 180°C fan/200°C/gas 6.

Tip the shallots, garlic, chillies, oil, sugar, sea salt and 5 cherry tomatoes into a food processor or high-speed blender and blitz until you have a rough paste.

Tip the aubergines and potatoes into a roasting tin large enough to hold them in one layer and mix with the spice paste. Top with the remaining whole cherry tomatoes, then transfer to the oven and roast for 45–50 minutes, until the aubergines and potatoes are cooked through.

Taste and season with lime juice and sea salt. Scatter over the coriander and serve with rice alongside.

Note: Depending on your spice tolerance, add or remove a fresh chilli from the spice paste. As always, this dish really does live or die by the seasoning you put on afterwards, so amend the lime and salt until it's just to your taste.

INDONESIAN COCONUT RICE, CRISPY CHILLI TOFU & PEANUT SAMBAL

This rice dish, known as nasi uduk in Indonesia, is rich with coconut, cloves, lemongrass and cassia. It's traditionalled served with fried shallots and a peanut sambal. Here, the shallots crisp up in the tray alongside. This is one of my favourite weeknight dishes.

Serves: 4
Prep: 15 minutes
Cook: 30 minutes

1 x 400ml tin of coconut milk
200g basmati rice, rinsed
1 stick of lemongrass, broken
5 cloves
1 piece of cassia/1 cinnamon stick
200g green beans,
   cut into 2cm pieces
3 banana/eschalion shallots,
   very thinly sliced
2 x 225g blocks of smoked
   or unsmoked firm tofu,
   cut into 1cm thick triangles
2 tablespoons sesame oil
1/2 red chilli, grated
2 cloves of garlic, grated
Sea salt flakes

SAMBAL
1 1/2 tablespoons crunchy
   peanut butter (about 75g)
1 1/2 tablespoons dark soy sauce
2 tablespoons lime juice
1/2 red chilli, grated
2-4 tablespoons water

TO SERVE
Fresh coriander, chopped

Preheat the oven to 210°C fan/230°C/gas 8.

Tip the coconut milk, rice, lemongrass, cloves, cassia or cinnamon stick and a pinch of sea salt flakes into a small lidded casserole dish or medium roasting tin, stir, then cover with the lid or tightly with foil (this is important so the rice cooks through) and set aside.

Tip the green beans, shallots and tofu into another roasting tin, large enough to just hold everything in one layer. Mix well with the sesame oil, chilli, grated garlic and 1/2 teaspoon of sea salt flakes. Make sure the tofu is on top so it can get crispy and transfer to the oven with the rice for 30 minutes, until the rice is cooked and the tofu, shallots and beans are crisp. (Check on the tofu after 20 minutes to make sure it doesn't burn.)

Meanwhile, mix together the peanut butter, soy sauce, lime juice and chilli and add the water as needed for a thin pouring consistency. Taste and adjust the lime juice and soy sauce.

Once cooked, scatter the tofu with the coriander and serve the rice and tofu with the sambal.

Note: You do need two tins for this dish – it is worth it for the contrast of the crisp tofu and shallots against the almost buttery rice.

ROASTED SPICED MUSHROOMS & PANEER WITH SQUASH, POMEGRANATE & MANGO

Texturally paneer and mushrooms work beautifully when simply roasted together with spices and squash. Along with the mango and pomegranate salsa, this is a flavoursome combination inspired by a New Zealand fusion dish I read about on holiday.

Serves: 3 to 4
Prep: 15 minutes
Cook: 35–40 minutes

225g paneer, cut into 2cm cubes
600g butternut squash,
   cut into 2cm cubes
250g chestnut mushrooms
1 x 400g tin of chickpeas, drained
2 tablespoons olive oil
1 tablespoon yogurt
2 $\frac{1}{2}$ cm ginger, peeled and grated
2 teaspoons ground coriander
2 teaspoons ground cumin
$\frac{1}{2}$ teaspoon ground turmeric
1 teaspoon chilli flakes
1 teaspoon sea salt flakes

SALSA
125g pomegranate seeds
1 mango, peeled
   and cut into small chunks
1 teaspoon brown sugar
10g fresh coriander or mint
1 teaspoon freshly ground
   black pepper
$\frac{1}{2}$ lime, zest and juice

TO SERVE
Naan bread and natural yogurt

Preheat the oven to 180°C fan/200°C/gas 6.

Tip the paneer, squash, mushrooms, (halved if large) chickpeas, olive oil, yogurt, grated ginger, spices and salt into one really large roasting tin (you want everything to fit in roughly one layer) and mix well. It's OK if the paneer sits on top of the other veg.

Transfer the tin to the oven and roast for 35–40 minutes, until the squash is cooked through, and the paneer is golden brown.

Meanwhile, mix together the pomegranate seeds, mango, brown sugar, coriander or mint, pepper and lime zest and juice. Serve the roasted paneer and vegetables piled into naan breads, with the salsa and yogurt alongside.

HOT-SMOKED SALMON FRITTATA
WITH YOGURT & DILL

This is a perfect brunch dish. By all means use smoked salmon if that's more readily available – I like the slightly gentler flavour that you get from hot-smoked salmon. The capers are entirely at your discretion.

Serves: 2
Prep: 10 minutes
Cook: 30–35 minutes

6 free-range eggs
200g natural yogurt
1/2 red onion, very finely chopped
20g fresh dill, roughly chopped
100–120g hot-smoked
  salmon flakes
1 teaspoon capers (optional)
Freshly ground black pepper

TO SERVE
A few tablespoons
  of natural yogurt

Preheat the oven to 150°C fan/170°C/gas 3.

Whisk the eggs and yogurt together, then stir through the onion and dill. Transfer to a small, shallow roasting tin lined with baking parchment (you want the egg mixture to fill the tin at least 2 1/2 cm deep). Scatter with the hot-smoked salmon flakes and capers, if using, season well with freshly ground black pepper, then transfer to the oven and bake for 30–35 minutes, until the egg has just set in the centre, but the frittata is ever so slightly wobbly.

Let the frittata sit for 10 minutes, then serve warm, with more natural yogurt alongside.

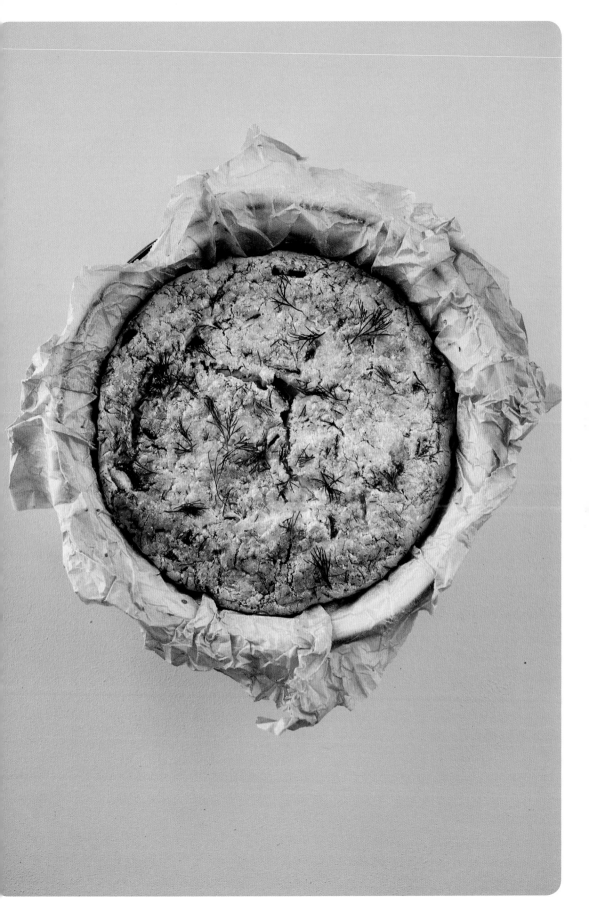

FILIPINO-STYLE VEGETABLE ADOBO WITH GARLIC & BAY

I first read about adobo, as with a lot of dishes, in Niki Segnit's *The Flavour Thesaurus* – a Filipino way of cooking meat, often pork, with vinegar, garlic and bay leaves. It also works beautifully as a way of cooking vegetables, and I love using the marinade here on crispy Tenderstem broccoli, the rather new and exciting long-stemmed cauliflower, and a good handful of shiitake mushrooms. (You can of course use ordinary broccoli and cauliflower.)

Serves: 2
Prep: 10 minutes
Cook: 25–30 minutes

300g Tenderstem broccoli
150g long-stemmed sprouting
   cauliflower or an ordinary small
   cauliflower, cut into florets
150g shiitake mushrooms, whole
3 cloves of garlic, grated
3 bay leaves
2 tablespoons sunflower
   or olive oil
2 tablespoons Chinese
   or white vinegar
1 tablespoon dark soy sauce

TO SERVE
3 spring onions, thinly sliced
Freshly cooked rice

Preheat the oven to 180°C fan/200°C/gas 6.

Tip the broccoli and cauliflower into a large bowl, then pour over a kettleful of boiling water. Let them sit for 2 minutes, then drain well and transfer the vegetables into a roasting tin large enough to hold everything in one layer.

Add the shiitake mushrooms, then mix through the garlic, bay leaves, oil, vinegar and soy sauce, making sure everything is well coated. Transfer to the oven and roast for 25–30 minutes, until the broccoli is crisp and slightly charred at the edges.

Taste and adjust the salt as needed, then scatter over the spring onions and serve with rice alongside.

SALTED CHOCOLATE & RASPBERRY LAMINGTONS

Lamingtons are a classic Australian cake – a simple sponge, topped with chocolate and coconut. Opinion is divided as to whether they should include jam – I rather like it with, so have included it here. A tiny bit of the country's favourite Vegemite adds a grown-up, salted edge to the dark chocolate ganache – I could happily eat half of these all by myself.

Serves: 4
Prep: 15 minutes
Cook: 25 minutes

115g caster sugar
115g softened unsalted butter
2 free-range eggs
115g self-raising flour
1 teaspoon baking powder
4 teaspoons raspberry jam

ICING
50g dark chocolate
  (minimum 70% cocoa solids)
25g unsalted butter
Scant 1/2 teaspoon Vegemite

TO DECORATE
A handful of coconut flakes

Preheat the oven to 160°C fan/180°C/gas 4.

Beat the sugar and butter together until softened, then whisk in the eggs, one at a time. Fold in the flour and baking powder, then transfer to an 26cm by 20cm lined baking tin and bake for 20–25 minutes, until the cake is golden brown on top, and a skewer inserted comes out clean.

Let the cake cool in the tin for 5 minutes, then on a wire rack until completely cold.

Cut the cake in half – not horizontally, which would be difficult for such a thin cake, but vertically across the middle – then sandwich the two halves together with the raspberry jam. Cut the cake into 6 even squares, and arrange on a plate or back in the tin.

Heat the chocolate, butter and Vegemite in a small saucepan until smooth and glossy, then carefully spoon a tablespoon over each sandwiched cake. Scatter over the coconut flakes, and serve when the icing has just set.

EUROPE & NORTH ASIA

EUROPE & NORTH ASIA

ALL-IN-ONE PAELLA WITH CHICKEN, PEPPERS & CHORIZO

ROAST CHICKEN WITH MUSHROOMS, CHICORY & DILL

HERBED CHICKEN WITH OLIVES,
ARTICHOKES & ROAST POTATOES

CROQUE MONSIEUR GRATIN WITH COMTÉ & PARMA HAM

CRISPY PESTO CHICKEN, ROASTED FENNEL & COURGETTES

ROSEMARY & HAZELNUT SALMON
WITH ROAST POTATOES & ASPARAGUS

RUSSIAN MEATBALLS
WITH SOUR CREAM, RICE & TOMATOES

SLOW ROASTED PEPPERS
WITH CHILLI, LEMON & GARLIC BEANS (VEGAN)

CRISPY HALLOUMI, ROASTED CARROTS, WALNUTS
& CANNELLINI BEANS (V)

STILTON, PEAR & WALNUT TART WITH ROSEMARY (V)

ROASTED BROCCOLI WITH PEAS, FETA,
BUTTER BEANS & QUINOA (V)

LEMON PEARL BARLEY RISOTTO WITH CHARD,
PARSLEY & ALMONDS (VEGAN)

AMARETTO ROASTED PLUMS, NECTARINES & PEACHES
WITH PISTACHIO GRANOLA (V)

ALL-IN-ONE PAELLA
WITH CHICKEN, PEPPERS & CHORIZO

Inspired by oven-cook risottos, I give you this oven-cooked paella – no stirring, just beautifully cooked saffron rice, rich with chorizo, chicken and garlic. While it's celebratory enough to serve to friends, I'd happily eat leftovers for the rest of the week's lunches or dinners – the flavour only improves overnight in the fridge.

Serves: 4
Prep: 10 minutes
Cook: 1 hour 25 minutes

1 red onion, roughly chopped
2 red peppers, thinly sliced
2 cloves of garlic, grated
6 free-range skinless, boneless
  chicken thighs
150g firm chorizo,
  thickly sliced into 1cm coins
2 tablespoons olive oil
4 generous pinches of good
  saffron (I like Belazu)
250g paella rice
600ml hot chicken stock
1 lemon, juice only
Sea salt flakes, to taste

TO SERVE
Chopped flat-leaf parsley
1 lemon, cut into wedges

Note: You could freeze and defrost this in portions if making ahead.

Preheat the oven to 180°C fan/200°C/gas 6.

Tip the onion, peppers, garlic, chicken thighs, chorizo and olive oil into a roasting tin or a flat lidded casserole dish large enough to hold everything in roughly one layer (it's OK if there's a bit of overlap). Transfer to the oven and roast for 25 minutes.

Meanwhile, pop the saffron strands into a mug with a couple of tablespoons of boiling water, and set aside.

Once the chicken and peppers have had 25 minutes, remove the tin from the oven and stir through the paella rice, hot chicken stock, and steeped saffron along with the saffron water. Cover tightly with foil or the lid (this is important so the rice cooks), then return the dish to the oven at 160°C fan/180°C/gas 4 for a further hour, until the rice is cooked through.

Once the paella is cooked, add a dash more hot chicken stock or boiling water to adjust the texture as you wish, squeeze over the lemon juice, taste and adjust the salt as needed, then serve hot, scattered with parsley and with lemon wedges alongside.

ROAST CHICKEN WITH MUSHROOMS, CHICORY & DILL

Chicken, dill and mushrooms are a perfect match for each other, and along with the mildly bitter chicory, they work beautifully with the creamy, lemon-spiked Puy lentils. A favourite of this book's photographer, David, and art director, Pene.

Serves: 4
Prep: 10 minutes
Cook: 1 hour

1kg free-range chicken thighs
   and drumsticks
500g chestnut mushrooms,
   whole
2 large heads of chicory,
   quartered
1 leek, thickly sliced
3 tablespoons olive oil
15–20g fresh dill
1 teaspoon sea salt flakes
Freshly ground black pepper
250g cooked vac-packed
   Puy lentils
300ml crème fraîche
Lemon juice, to taste

TO SERVE
Crusty bread

Preheat the oven to 180°C fan/200°C/gas 6.

Tip the chicken, mushrooms, chicory and leek into a roasting tin large enough to hold everything in one layer (but don't worry if the chicken has to sit on top of the vegetables). Mix through the olive oil and three-quarters of the dill, then scatter with the sea salt flakes and freshly ground black pepper. Transfer to the oven and roast for 50 minutes.

After 50 minutes, scatter the Puy lentils evenly over the vegetables, then dot the crème fraîche all over and gently stir it in, taking care not to get any on the crispy chicken skin. Return the tin to the oven for a further 10 minutes, until the crème fraîche is bubbling.

Let the tin rest out of the oven for 10 minutes, then squeeze the lemon juice over the chicken and vegetables to taste, scatter with the remaining fresh dill and serve hot, with crusty bread on the side.

HERBED CHICKEN WITH OLIVES, ARTICHOKES & ROAST POTATOES

I love the combination of artichokes, olives and chicken – and with potatoes, tomatoes and plenty of herbs, this easy weekend traybake has everything you would want for a lazy weekend lunch, all in one tin. Excellent fuel for a long afternoon dog-walk.

Serves: 4
Prep: 15 minutes
Cook: 1 hour

800g Charlotte potatoes, halved
1 red onion, quartered
8 tomatoes on the vine
8 free-range chicken thighs
  and drumsticks
1 lemon, cut into eighths
1 x 280g jar of artichokes in oil,
  drained (keep the oil)
2 teaspoons sea salt flakes
Freshly ground black pepper
3–4 sprigs of fresh rosemary
5–6 sprigs of fresh thyme
1 x 340g jar of pitted black olives,
  drained
1/2 lemon, zest and juice
20g flat-leaf parsley,
  finely chopped

Preheat the oven to 180°C fan/200°C/gas 6.

Tip the potatoes, onion, tomatoes, chicken and lemon into a tin large enough to hold everything in one layer, and mix it all well with the oil from the jar of artichokes. (This might seem like a lot of oil, but the potatoes can take it.)

Scatter everything – particularly the chicken – with the sea salt and black pepper, then tip the fresh herbs over, transfer to the oven and roast for 1 hour.

Meanwhile, mix the drained artichokes and olives with the lemon juice, zest and parsley. Tip these into the roasting tin over the potatoes for the last 15 minutes to warm through, then let the chicken rest for 10 minutes before serving hot.

CROQUE MONSIEUR GRATIN
WITH COMTÉ & PARMA HAM

This dish will make your house and kitchen smell like you're a legitimate domestic goddess – forget the pot of fresh coffee if you're trying to sell your house, I'd certainly move in if this hit me when I opened the front door. It's unashamedly indulgent, and I'd serve it for brunch (alongside that coffee and some fruit), or for a weekend dinner along with a crisp green salad.

Serves: 4, generously
Prep: 15 minutes, plus
          15 minutes resting
Cook: 25 minutes

8 all-butter croissants, halved
200g Comté, grated
500ml crème fraîche
6 free-range eggs, lightly beaten
1 teaspoon smooth Dijon mustard
Plenty of freshly ground
  black pepper
80g Parma ham

TO SERVE
Chopped flat-leaf parsley

Preheat the oven to 180°C fan/200°C/gas 6.

Stuff the halved croissants with the grated Comté, and arrange them in a roasting tin or ovenproof dish large and deep enough to fit them all snugly.

Beat the crème fraîche, eggs, Dijon mustard and pepper together, and pour half of this over the croissants in the roasting tin. It will look like you have far too much crème fraîche mix, but be patient – squash the first lot down over the croissants and leave it to absorb for 15 minutes.

Once it's almost absorbed, pour the remaining mixture over, arrange the Parma ham on the top as you wish, then transfer to the oven and bake for 25 minutes, until crisp and golden brown.

Scatter over the chopped parsley and serve.

CRISPY PESTO CHICKEN, ROASTED FENNEL & COURGETTES

This is such an easy weeknight dinner – I love the combination of the simply roasted vegetables alongside the crisp, flavoursome chicken. The courgettes work really well with the peppers and fennel.

Serves: 4
Prep: 15 minutes
Cook: 45 minutes

3 mixed peppers, thickly sliced
2 courgettes, thickly sliced
1 red onion, thickly sliced
2 small or 1 large bulb
  of fennel (approx. 300g),
  roughly chopped
2 tablespoons olive oil
1 teaspoon sea salt flakes
A handful of fresh sage leaves
4 free-range chicken breasts
4 heaped teaspoons fresh pesto
  (I like the chilled kind you
  get next to the ravioli at
  the supermarket)
4 heaped tablespoons panko
  or white breadcrumbs
A couple of handfuls of spinach,
  roughly chopped

Preheat the oven to 180°C fan/200°C/gas 6

Tip the vegetables, oil, sea salt and sage leaves into a roasting tin large enough to hold everything in one layer, mix well, then transfer to the oven and roast for 20 minutes.

After the veg have had 20 minutes, make space in the tin for the chicken breasts. Spread each one with a teaspoon of fresh pesto, scatter over the panko or fresh breadcrumbs, then pop the tray back into the oven for a further 25–30 minutes, until the breadcrumbs are golden brown and the chicken is cooked through. Add the chopped spinach, let the chicken rest for 5 minutes, then serve hot, with a little more sea salt if needed.

Note: The cooking time for the chicken will vary depending on the size of the chicken breasts – if they are small to ordinary size, 20 minutes for the veg plus 25 minutes for the chicken as above will be fine. If you've gone to the butcher and have got supersize ones, make it 15 minutes to start off for the veg, and 35 minutes with the chicken on top.

ROSEMARY & HAZELNUT SALMON WITH ROAST POTATOES & ASPARAGUS

I pulled this dish together from a fridge forage with about ten minutes to spare before a girlfriend came over for dinner – it was so ridiculously nice for how little time I had taken on it. While asparagus, potatoes and salmon are a classic combination, they reach happy new heights here along with hazelnuts and copious amounts of garlic and rosemary.

Serves: 2
Prep: 15 minutes
Cook: 40 minutes

300g Charlotte potatoes,
    quartered
2 cloves of garlic, finely grated
2 sprigs of fresh rosemary,
    roughly chopped
3 tablespoons olive oil
1 1/2 teaspoons sea salt flakes
1 lemon, zest only
1 small clove of garlic,
    finely grated
2 nice salmon fillets
200–250g asparagus
    (tips are fine if the whole ones
    look woody)
100g blanched hazelnuts,
    roughly chopped

DRESSING
4 heaped tablespoons good
    natural yogurt
1/2 lemon, juice only

Preheat the oven to 180°C fan/200°C/gas 6.

Tip the potatoes, the garlic, and the rosemary, 2 tablespoons of the olive oil and 1 teaspoon of sea salt flakes into a roasting tin large enough to hold everything in one layer, then transfer to the oven and roast for 20 minutes.

Meanwhile, mix the lemon zest, garlic, olive oil and remaining sea salt flakes in a shallow bowl and gently coat the salmon and asparagus. Set aside.

Once the potatoes have had 20 minutes, lower the oven to 160°C fan/180°C/gas 4. Make space for the salmon fillets in the tin and lay the asparagus over the potatoes. Scatter over the hazelnuts, then return to the oven for a further 20 minutes, until the salmon is just cooked through and the asparagus is crisp.

Mix the yogurt and lemon juice together, and serve alongside the salmon, potatoes and asparagus.

Note: If you can't find Charlottes, use potatoes like Maris Piper or King Edward, cut into 2 1/2 cm chunks.

RUSSIAN MEATBALLS
WITH SOUR CREAM, RICE & TOMATOES

These meatballs, known as tefteli in Russia, are a delight – instead of adding breadcrumbs to the mince, you add a handful of cooked long-grain rice, so they're often known as 'porcupine' meatballs, The sour cream and tomato sauce works beautifully with the base of softened onions and carrots – this is a firm weekend favourite.

Serves: 4
Prep: 15 minutes
Cook: 35 minutes

MEATBALLS
1 small carrot, peeled and grated
1 small onion, peeled
  and roughly chopped
15g fresh dill (reserve a tiny
  bit to scatter over at the end)
400g beef mince
400g pork mince
2 teaspoons sea salt flakes
1 free-range egg
4 heaped tablespoons
  cooked long-grain rice

SAUCE
1 onion, finely chopped
1 carrot, peeled and grated
1 tablespoon butter
1 tablespoon olive oil
2 x 400g tins of chopped
  tomatoes
2 cloves of garlic, finely grated
150g sour cream

TO SERVE
Cooked long-grain rice
  or mashed potato

Preheat the oven to 180°C fan/200°C/gas 6.

Before you start on the meatballs, tip the onion, carrot, butter and olive oil for the sauce into a large roasting tin, and transfer to the oven for 7–10 minutes to soften.

Meanwhile, pop the other carrot and onion, dill, mince, sea salt flakes and egg into a food processor, and blitz until well blended. Stir through the rice, then set aside.

Stir the tinned tomatoes, garlic and sour cream into the roasting tin. With wet hands, form the mince into about 24 meatballs the size of table tennis balls, and arrange them over the sauce. Transfer the tin to the oven, and roast for 30–35 minutes, until the meatballs are golden brown, and the sauce is slightly reduced.

Scatter with fresh dill and serve with rice.

NOTE: Because I don't want to make a panful of rice when only a few tablespoons are needed, I tend to microwave ready-cooked Tilda rice in a packet for this dish.

SLOW ROASTED PEPPERS
WITH CHILLI, LEMON & GARLIC BEANS

My favourite dish when working in a restaurant kitchen was peperonata – red and yellow peppers softened down slowly in a frying pan along with oil, garlic and onions until they almost melted. It was, as many good things are, time-consuming to make, so I wondered if one might achieve a similar result with oven cooking – and the answer is yes. With garlicky beans, this dish is perfect piled on to rounds of thickly sliced toasted bread.

Serves: 4
Prep: 15 minutes
Cook: 1 hour

5 vine tomatoes, quartered
1 red pepper, thinly sliced
1 yellow pepper, thinly sliced
1 orange pepper, thinly sliced
2 tablespoons olive oil
2 bay leaves
1 large sprig of fresh rosemary
1/2 – 1 teaspoon sea salt flakes
Plenty of freshly ground
  black pepper

BEANS
2 tablespoons extra virgin olive oil
1/2 clove of garlic, finely grated
1/2 teaspoon chilli flakes
1/2 – 1 teaspoon sea salt flakes
1 x 400g tin of cannellini beans,
  drained and rinsed
1/2 lemon, zest only

TO SERVE
Rounds of thickly sliced,
  toasted bread

Preheat the oven to 180°C fan/200°C/gas 6.

Tip the tomatoes, peppers, oil, herbs, salt and pepper into a roasting tin large enough to hold everything in one layer, mix well, then transfer to the oven and roast for 50 minutes. If after half an hour it looks as though the peppers are catching a bit too quickly, turn the heat down a fraction.

Meanwhile, stir the extra virgin olive oil, garlic, chilli flakes, salt, cannellini beans and lemon zest together in a bowl and set aside. Once the peppers have had 50 minutes, stir through the beans, then turn the oven down to 160°C fan/180°C/gas 4 and cook for a further 10 minutes.

Taste and adjust the salt and pepper as needed, adding a little more olive oil if you wish, then remove the bay leaves and rosemary sprigs and serve piled on to toasted bread. This tastes even better the next day, so it's well worth making in advance and reheating.

CRISPY HALLOUMI, ROASTED CARROTS, WALNUTS & CANNELLINI BEANS

I love the combination of crisp, salty halloumi against lemon-spiked cannellini beans and sweet roasted carrots. This warm salad would be as perfect for a weeknight dinner with a pile of flatbreads as it would be alongside other salads for a weekend lunch spread.

Serves: 3–4
Prep: 15 minutes
Cook: 30 minutes

300g baby carrots, whole
225g halloumi,
    cut into ½ cm slices
1 red onion, cut into eighths
A handful of lemon thyme
1 teaspoon ground cumin
2 tablespoons olive oil
1 x 400g tin of cannellini beans,
    drained
50g walnuts, roughly chopped
2 tablespoons extra virgin olive oil
1 tablespoon honey
½ lemon, zest and juice
½ teaspoon sea salt
100g rocket

TO SERVE
Thick Greek yogurt and flatbreads

Preheat the oven to 180°C fan/200°C/gas 6.

Tip the baby carrots, halloumi and red onion into a roasting tin large enough to hold everything in one layer, then mix through the lemon thyme, cumin and olive oil. Transfer to the oven and roast for 30–35 minutes, until the halloumi is golden brown, and the carrots are just cooked through.

While the halloumi and carrots are in the oven, mix the beans, walnuts, extra virgin olive oil, honey, orange zest and juice and salt and set aside.

Stir the beans and rocket through the roasted carrots and halloumi, and serve with yogurt and flatbreads alongside.

Note: This is at its best eaten immediately, while the halloumi is still hot, but if you have leftovers it's not at all bad in a lunchbox the next day.

STILTON, PEAR & WALNUT TART
WITH ROSEMARY

A cookbook solely comprised of puff pastry tarts was mooted as we took the photograph opposite, and it's not hard to see why – there's such an infinite variety of interesting things you can use to top them. Stilton, pears and walnuts are a classic combination, and this dish makes a wonderful dinner party starter or light lunch along with a green salad.

Serves: 4
Prep: 10 minutes
Cook: 30 minutes

3 pears, cut into $\frac{1}{2}$ cm slices
1 x 420g sheet of all-butter
   puff pastry
2 sprigs of fresh rosemary,
   needles finely chopped
125g vegetarian Stilton, crumbled
50g walnuts, roughly chopped
1 heaped tablespoon honey

Preheat the oven to 180°C fan/200°C/gas 6.

Arrange the sliced pears over the pastry, then scatter over the rosemary and Stilton. Transfer to the oven and bake for 20 minutes.

After 20 minutes, scatter over the chopped walnuts and evenly drizzle the honey over the tart. Return it to the oven for a further 10 minutes, until the pastry is golden brown and crisp, and the walnuts are just toasted.

ROASTED BROCCOLI WITH PEAS, FETA, BUTTER BEANS & QUINOA

This dish is as good for a weeknight dinner as it is for a lunchbox the next day, and feels nicely balanced with the broccoli, peas and butter beans against the feta, quinoa and lemon.

Serves: 4
Prep: 10 minutes
Cook: 30 minutes

125g quinoa
325ml water
1 x 400g tin of butter beans,
    drained
1 large head of broccoli,
    cut into large florets
150g frozen peas
200g feta cheese, crumbled
40g flaked almonds
15g mint leaves,
    roughly chopped
A few teaspoons of pink
    peppercorns (optional)

DRESSING
4 tablespoons extra virgin olive oil
2 lemons, zest and juice
Lots of freshly ground
    black pepper
1 teaspoon sea salt flakes

Preheat the oven to 180°C fan/200°C/gas 6.

Tip the quinoa, water and butter beans into a roasting tin or lidded casserole dish, then arrange the broccoli on top in a single layer, and scatter over the frozen peas. Cover tightly with foil or the lid, then transfer to the oven and roast for 30 minutes.

Meanwhile, whisk the olive oil, lemon zest and juice and freshly ground black pepper together with the sea salt. Once the broccoli and quinoa are just cooked through, drizzle with the dressing, scatter over the feta, almonds, mint and peppercorns, if using, and serve hot or at room temperature.

LEMON PEARL BARLEY RISOTTO
WITH CHARD, PARSLEY & ALMONDS

With ordinary risottos, I always think the magic happens when you add the Parmesan at the end; in this vegan version, almond butter does the same job, for a dish which is so warming and rich you'd be hard pressed to know it was completely plant-based. A lovely midweek or weekend dinner.

Serves: 4
Prep: 10 minutes
Cook: 45 minutes

200g pearl barley
500ml boiling vegetable stock
1 clove of garlic, unpeeled
1 white onion, finely chopped
250g rainbow chard,
   cut into 1cm slices
1 lemon, zest and juice
   plus the squeezed lemon halves
1 tablespoon extra virgin olive oil
30g almond butter
20g finely chopped flat-leaf
   parsley
30g whole blanched almonds
Sea salt and freshly ground
   black pepper

TO SERVE
Unsweetened non-dairy yogurt,
   or ricotta (if you aren't vegan)

Preheat the oven to 180°C fan/200°C/gas 6.

Tip the pearl barley, stock, garlic, onion and chard into a roasting tin or lidded casserole dish along with the squeezed lemon halves. Cover tightly with foil or the lid, then transfer to the oven and bake for 45 minutes.

Meanwhile, mix the lemon zest, juice, olive oil, almond butter and parsley together and set aside.

When the risotto has just 10 minutes left to cook, pop the almonds on a baking tray, scatter over a pinch of sea salt and slide them in alongside to toast.

Stir the parsley, lemon and almond butter mixture through the risotto, then taste and adjust the salt and pepper as needed. You may wish to add a tiny bit more boiling water to loosen it – if so, do taste and season again afterwards.

Serve the risotto with a spoon of non-dairy yogurt or ricotta and scatter the toasted almonds on top.

AMARETTO ROASTED PLUMS, NECTARINES & PEACHES WITH PISTACHIO GRANOLA

A dash of amaretto gives the gently roasted peaches, plums and nectarines in this dish the most wonderful almond flavour, but you could easily substitute elderflower liqueur or whatever you have handy in the cupboard. Cooking the granola in a tin alongside keeps it nice and crisp. This is a perfect late summer or early autumn pudding along with a spoonful of mascarpone or vegan ice cream.

Serves: 4–6
Prep: 10 minutes
Cook: 25 minutes

4 peaches or nectarines, halved
4 flat peaches, whole
4 plums, halved
  (or a mixture of your favourite
  orchard fruit)
6 tablespoons soft light
  brown sugar
200ml amaretto liqueur
60g flaked almonds
40g oats
50g pistachios, lightly chopped
30ml olive oil

TO SERVE
Vegan ice cream or mascarpone

Preheat the oven to 140°C fan/160°C/gas 3. (This might seem low, but you want the fruit to cook very gently.)

Arrange the fruit in a roasting tin large enough to hold everything in one layer, scatter over 4 tablespoons of the brown sugar, then pour over the amaretto liqueur. Transfer to the oven and roast for 25 minutes, until the fruit is just soft. (If your fruit is very under-ripe, it may take slightly longer.)

Meanwhile, mix the flaked almonds, oats, pistachios, olive oil and the remaining 2 tablespoons of brown sugar and spread them out on a separate baking tray. Pop them alongside the tray of fruit and roast for 20 minutes, until just crisp.

Serve the fruit hot, with vegan ice cream or mascarpone alongside, scattered with the granola. Leftovers are excellent for breakfast with yogurt too.

BIBLIOGRAPHY

For further reading, I've suggested my favourite books organised by country, but starting with a general list.

GENERAL
Bourdain, Anthony, *A Cook's Tour: Global Adventures in Extreme Cuisines*, Ecco, 2002.
Gilbert, Sandra M., *The Culinary Imagination: from Myth to Modernity*, Norton, 2014.
Nosrat, Samin, *Salt, Fat, Acid, Heat*, Canongate, 2017.
Segnit, Niki, *The Flavour Thesaurus*, Bloomsbury, 2015.
Segnit, Niki, *Lateral Cooking*, Bloomsbury, 2019.

CENTRAL AND SOUTH AMERICA
Acurio, Gastón, and Andy Sewell, *Peru: The Cookbook*, Phaidon, 2015.
Gálvez, Madelaine Vázquez, and Imogene Tondre, *Cuba: the Cookbook*, Phaidon, 2018.
Iyer, Rukmini, *M is for Mexican*, Quadrille, 2016.
Miers, Thomasina, *Wahaca: Mexican Food at Home*, Hodder & Stoughton, 2012.
Presilla, Maricel, *Gran Cocina Latina: The Food of Latin America*, Norton, 2012.
Stein, Rick, *The Road to Mexico*, BBC Books, 2017.

USA AND THE CARIBBEAN
Colwin, Laurie, *Home Cooking*, Fig Tree, 2012.
Ephron, Nora, *Heartburn*, Virago, 2008.
Harriott, Ainsley, *Ainsley's Caribbean Kitchen*, Ebury, 2019.
Iyer, Rukmini, *C is for Caribbean*, Quadrille, 2017.
Keller, Thomas, *The French Laundry Cookbook*, Workman, 1999.
Kingsolver, Barbara, *Animal, Vegetable, Miracle: A Year of Food Life*, Harper, 2007.
Ramoutar, Shivi, *Caribbean Modern*, Headline, 2015.
Remnick, David, et al., *Secret Ingredients: The New Yorker Book of Food and Drink*, Modern Library, 2008.
Severson, Kim, *Spoon Fed*, Riverhead, 2011.

ASIA
Ahmed, Saliha Mahmood, *Khazana: An Indo-Persian Cookbook*, Hodder & Stoughton, 2018.
Anderson, Tim, *Tokyo Stories: A Japanese Cookbook*, Hardie Grant, 2019.
Bourke, Jordan and Regina Pyo, *Our Korean Kitchen*, W&N, 2015.
Chan, Kei Lum and Diora Fong Chan, *China: the Cookbook*, Phaidon, 2016.
Dunlop, Fuchsia, *Every Grain of Rice: Simple Chinese Home Cooking*, Bloomsbury, 2012.
Dunlop, Fuchsia, *The Food of Sichuan*, Bloomsbury, 2019.
Iyer, Rukmini, *K is for Korean*, Quadrille, 2016.
Iyer, Rukmini, *S is for Sri Lankan*, Quadrille, 2017.
Jaffrey, Madhur, *Indian Cooking*, BBC Books, 1992.

Kim, Emily, *Maangchi's Real Korean Cooking: Authentic Dishes for the Home Cook*, Rux Martin/ Houghton Mifflin Harcourt, 2015.

Razdan, Sarla, *Kashmiri Cuisine: Through the Ages,* Roli Books, 2011.

Sarkhel, Udit and Simon Parkes, *The Calcutta Kitchen*, Mitchell Beazley, 2006.

Sodha, Meera, *East: 120 Vegan and Vegetarian Recipes from Bangalore to Beijing*, Fig Tree, 2019.

AFRICA AND THE MIDDLE EAST

Ottolenghi, Yotam and Sami Tamimi, *Jerusalem*, Ebury, 2012.

Ottolenghi, Yotam, *Plenty*, Ebury, 2010.

Roden, Claudia, *The Book of Jewish Food*, Penguin, 1999.

Roden, Claudia, *A New Book of Middle Eastern Food*, Penguin, 1986.

Aribisala, Yemisi, *Longthroat Memoirs*, Cassava, 2016.

Adjonyoh, Zoe, *Zoe's Ghana Kitchen*, Mitchell Beazley, 2017.

Ariyo, Lopè, *Hibiscus: Discover Fresh Flavours from West Africa*, Mitchell Beazley, 2017.

SOUTH EAST ASIA AND AUSTRALASIA

Basan, Ghillie, *Classic Recipes of the Philippines*, Lorenz, 2015.

Chio-Lauri, Jacqueline, *The New Filipino Kitchen*, Agate Surrey, 2018.

Coombes, Ping, *Malaysia: Recipes from a Family Kitchen*, W&N, 2016

Ford, Eleanor, *Fire Islands: Recipes from Indonesia*, Murdoch, 2019.

Greenwood, Helen, *The Great Australian Cookbook*, Blackwell & Ruth, 2019.

Harper, Tim and Murray Thom, *The Great New Zealand Cookbook*, Blackwell & Ruth, 2019.

Luu, Uyen, *My Vietnamese Kitchen*, Ryland Peters & Small, 2013.

Musa, Norman, *Amazing Malaysian*, Square Peg, 2016.

Nguyen, Andrea, *Vietnamese Food Any Day*, Ten Speed Press, 2019.

Owen, Sri, *Sri Owen's Indonesian Food*, Pavilion, 2015.

Thompson, David, *Thai Food*, Pavilion, 2002.

EUROPE AND NORTH ASIA

Andres, Jose, *Tapas: A Taste of Spain in America*, Clarkson Potter, 2005.

David, Elizabeth, *Italian Food*, Folio Society, 1998.

Colquhoun, Kate, *Taste: The Story of Britain through Its Cooking*, Bloomsbury, 2008.

Hayden, Georgina, *Taverna*, Square Peg, 2019.

Historic England Archive, *Food and Cooking in Britain*, English Heritage, 1992.

Khoo, Rachel, *The Little Swedish Kitchen*, Michael Joseph, 2018.

Schuhbeck, Alfons, *The German Cookbook*, Phaidon, 2018.

Timoshkina, Alissa, *Salt and Time: Recipes from a Modern Russian Kitchen*, Mitchell Beazley, 2019

INDEX

ABOUT THE AUTHOR

Rukmini Iyer is the bestselling author of the *Roasting Tin* Series. She is a recipe writer, food stylist and formerly a lawyer. She loves creating delicious and easy recipes with minimum fuss and maximum flavour. Rukmini believes family dinners are an integral part of the day and is passionate about helping people make it possible.

Rukmini grew up in Cambridgeshire with the best of three food cultures: Bengali and South Indian food from her parents' Indian heritage, along with classic 80s mac & cheese, sponge puddings and cheese & pineapple on sticks. Rukmini's career began with a training contract at a leading law firm, but she realised that as she spent all day thinking about food, all evening cooking, and most of her law lectures or time in the office scribbling down ideas for new dishes in the margins of her notebook, a career in food was a sensible move. She decided to retrain as a food stylist, so after cookery school and a summer working at a Michelin-starred restaurant to learn the ropes, she began work as a food stylist. Surrounded by food all day on photo shoots, she noticed the meals she made at home grew simpler, often just in a roasting tin, and that there were ways of packing in flavour and interest to the dishes with an absolute minimum effort - this became the inspiration for the series.

As well as writing cookbooks, Rukmini styles and writes recipes for numerous brands and publications, including Waitrose, *The Guardian* and Fortnum & Mason. When not working with food, she can usually be found walking her beautiful border collie Pepper by the riverside in East London, entertaining at home or filling her balcony and flat with more plants than they can hold. Rukmini runs an occasional series of supper-clubs for charities including Oxfam and Women's Aid.

 @missminifer   @missminifer

A book is always a massive team effort. My thanks go as ever to my editor Rowan Yapp for her advice and friendship over the course of the book; to Lucie Cuthbertson-Twiggs for looking after both Pepper and myself on press trips; and to Faye, Rachel, Richard and the whole team at Vintage for their incredible support on the books.

The stunning design and art direction of the book are again all down to Pene Parker: thank you for making the book look so beautiful, being brilliant to work with as ever, and for taking Pepper on walks during the shoot. David Loftus, you have taken absolutely stunning photographs of the food as always, your work makes the books what they are: thank you so much for your support, and for taking such beautiful photographs of Pepper as well as going out mudlarking with her. Jo Jackson, thank you for your brilliant help on the shoot, recipe-testing and cooking the most beautiful versions of the food from the books as canapés, as well as looking after Pepper (there seems to be a theme here). Annie Lee, thank you for your helpful and eagle-eyed copy edit, and to Clare Sayer for an excellent proof-read.

This should have been in all my books, but the biggest inspiration for my recipes comes from Niki Segnit and her spectacular book, _The Flavour Thesaurus,_ and more recently, _Lateral Cooking_. At any point when I'm lost for ideas, staring at a broccoli and yelling 'But what do I DO with you?' I end up turning to the (by now concerned) dog, and reassure her out loud that it'll all be OK, we'll consult the books.

Thanks to Danielle Adams, Christine Beck, Emma Drage, Laura Hutchinson and Ruby Tandoh for amazing friendship, support and not least recipe-testing – your advice on the dishes is absolutely invaluable, as well as your combined ability to keep me (relatively) sane.

Rosie Breckner, I owe you incredible thanks, this book would not have happened without that conversation at your dining table, and you should seriously consider life or career coaching as a sideline from being a superstar mum and financier.

As always, my biggest thanks go to my family: Parvati, Vijay and Padmini. As well as all your unwavering love and support, Mum, thank you for stellar and often very late-notice recipe-testing. Dad, thank you for your excellent advice on the books and feedback on the dishes. Padz, tempting as it is to say 'not you', yet again, that was not bad work on the marked-up recipes. You know I really do appreciate your strong and stable (LOL! see what I did there) influence.

Pepper, as a border collie with an alarmingly quick rate of learning, I don't doubt that you'll be reading by the end of the year, so thank you for being a very good girl and for your helpful and nuanced recipe feedback. And yes, we can go for a walk now.

10 9 8 7 6

Square Peg, an imprint of Vintage,
20 Vauxhall Bridge Road,
London SW1V 2SA

Square Peg is part of the Penguin Random House group
of companies whose addresses can be found at:
global.penguinrandomhouse.com.
Text copyright © Rukmini Iyer 2020

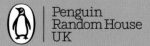

Rukmini Iyer has asserted her right to be identified as
the author of this Work in accordance with the Copyright,
Designs and Patents Act 1988

First published by Square Peg in 2020
Penguin.co.uk/vintage

A CIP catalogue record for this book is available
from the British Library
ISBN 9781529110135

Design & prop styling by Pene Parker
Photography by David Loftus
Map design by Sarah Greeno
Portrait by Urzula Soltys
Food styling by Rukmini Iyer
Food styling assistance by Jo Jackson
Printed and bound in Italy by L.E.G.O. S.p.A.

Penguin Random House is committed to a sustainable future
for our business, our readers and our planet.
This book is made from Forest Stewardship Council® certified paper.

THE ROASTING TIN
SIMPLE ONE DISH DINNERS
RUKMINI IYER

THE GREEN ROASTING TIN
VEGAN & VEGETARIAN ONE DISH DINNERS
RUKMINI IYER

THE QUICK ROASTING TIN
30 MINUTE ONE DISH DINNERS
RUKMINI IYER

THE ROASTING TIN AROUND THE WORLD
GLOBAL ONE DISH DINNERS
RUKMINI IYER

AVAILABLE NOW